Negotiation for Entrepreneurship

Negotiation for Entrepreneurship: Achieving a Successful Outcome

Vimal Babu and Robert Hisrich

ANTHEM PRESS

Anthem Press
An imprint of Wimbledon Publishing Company
www.anthempress.com

This edition first published in UK and USA 2023
by ANTHEM PRESS
75–76 Blackfriars Road, London SE1 8HA, UK
or PO Box 9779, London SW19 7ZG, UK
and
244 Madison Ave #116, New York, NY 10016, USA

British Library Cataloguing-in-Publication Data
A catalogue record for this book is available from the British Library.

Library of Congress Control Number: 2022914108
A catalog record for this book has been requested.

ISBN-13: 978-1-78527-776-4 (Hbk)
ISBN-10: 1-78527-776-6 (Hbk)
ISBN-13: 978-1-78527-779-5 (Pbk)
ISBN-10: 1-78527-779-0 (Pbk)

This title is also available as an e-book.

CONTENTS

PART III

Strategy, Planning and Tactics in Negotiation   **101**

ACKNOWLEDGMENTS

I owe a lot of thanks to everyone who have helped me with this textbook. I really appreciate the conscientious and useful insights, contributions and suggestions from my coauthor and eminent Chair Professor of International Marketing, Kent State University, Ohio, USA, Prof. (Dr) Robert Hisrich. Indeed, it was full of umpteen learning experiences working with you.

At Anthem Press, I thank the Acquisition and Editorial Support team including Jebaslin Hephzibah, Courtney Young, Basheer Ahmed and Megan Greiving for their constant support. Thanks to the worldwide Anthem Press sales team, without whose tireless efforts this textbook would have rested on a shelf.

To thank my family at home, I would first and foremost acknowledge my mother Jayasree, my father Babu Kumar, my wife Parvathy (Ammu) for her unwavering support, my son Aditya (Aadi) for his insatiable curiosity to find out more about the "how" aspect of the textbook and, of course, my brother Vipin and sister Veena for motivating constantly and keeping me always in high feather.

DEDICATED TO

Our families, students and all those who want to experience negotiation in an entrepreneurial environment.

ABOUT THE AUTHORS

The textbook is written by Vimal Babu and Robert Hisrich.

Vimal Babu, PhD

Vimal Babu, PhD, Associate Professor of Management with SRM University, Amaravati, India, works in the academic area of organizational behavior and entrepreneurship. His research interests lie in the intersection of leadership, negotiation, strategy and entrepreneurship. He previously worked for the Symbiosis Institute of Business Management (SIBM), Symbiosis International University, Pune, India, as Associate Professor. His passion for negotiation and conflict management reflects in the roles he has been playing as a negotiation expert and trainer. He regularly imparts leadership and negotiation training to corporate executives on Business Negotiation, Contract Negotiation, Conflict Management, Strategic Leadership, Building High-Performance Teams, inter alia. His research publications are with ABDC and *Scopus-Indexed International* journals. He is certified in Negotiation and Conflict Management from the Asian Institute of Management (AIM), Manila, Philippines, and the United States Institute of Peace (USIP). He also serves as a reviewer for nine ABDC-listed international journals. He received his PhD from the Centre for Management Studies, Jamia Millia Islamia (JMI) Central University, New Delhi, India.

Robert D. Hisrich, PhD

Robert D. Hisrich, PhD, former Director of the Walker Center of Global Entrepreneurship at Thunderbird School of Global Management, received his BA in English and Science from DePauw University and his MBA and PhD in Business Administration with a major in marketing from the University of Cincinnati. Hisrich also holds honorary doctorate degrees from Chuvash State University (Russia) and the University of Miskolc (Hungary). At present, he is associated with the College of Business and Administration, Kent State

University, Ohio, USA, as Bridgestone Chair of International Marketing and Director of The Global Management Center and International Programs.

His global experience includes being a visiting and honorary professor at more than eight universities in six different countries. Prof. (Dr) Hisrich has authored or coauthored 36 books, including *International Entrepreneurship: Starting, Developing, and Managing a Global Venture* (3rd edition) published by Sage Publications. His other books include *Corporate Entrepreneurship, Technology Entrepreneurship: Value Creation, Protection, and Capture* (2nd edition), *Governpreneurship: Establishing a Thriving Entrepreneurial Spirit in Your Government, Entrepreneurship: Starting, Developing, and Managing a New Enterprise* (translated into 13 languages and now in its ninth edition), *Entrepreneurial Finance: A Global Perspective and Marketing for Entrepreneurs* and *SMEs: An International Approach.*

Prof. (Dr) Hisrich has written more than 300 articles on entrepreneurship, international business management and marketing, which have appeared in such journals as *The Academy of Management Review, Strategic Management Journal, American Psychologist, California Management Review, Journal of Business Venturing, Sloan Management Review, Journal of Marketing* and *Journal of Marketing Research.*

FOREWORD

It gives me great pleasure to write the foreword to this excellent book by Dr Vimal Babu and Dr Robert Hisrich. I have known both authors and particularly Dr Babu through their extensive academic and research endeavors, as well as their international consulting work.

When I look back on my career, I realize that a person's *potential* to solve problems and overcome obstacles is not in itself enough to make a contribution. Rather, to leave a mark, this potential must be harnessed and given expression through effective human behavior. After more than two decades of professional experience, I am convinced that good negotiation is a particularly important aspect of human behavior that can favorably influence the outcomes attained by an individual.

Moreover, it doesn't matter whether you're negotiating with a person from a different field or industry, what matters is how you structure your negotiation to meet your needs. This is particularly true for entrepreneurs. Entrepreneurs have to deal with a variety of different stakeholders in the context of their work. As a result, they have to be adept at negotiating when they collaborate with others and need to accomplish their goals through the involvement, commitment and engagement of others. Entrepreneurs are savvy negotiators when they can persuade, influence and convince people with enhanced trustworthiness, transparency and authenticity in their actions and responses.

There is a lot in this book to recommend to readers. There are chapters on the basics of entrepreneurship, conflict management and communication, as well as the psychological and behavioral dimensions of being an entrepreneur. There are also chapters on negotiation and entrepreneurial ventures that cover topics such as the process of negotiation, considerations for entrepreneurs who are women and how cultural diversity affects how entrepreneurs negotiate. In general, the authors have done well in selecting the most essential aspects of negotiation in the context of entrepreneurship with a focus on evidence-based discussions, real-life examples, case scenarios and thought-provoking questions as well as a rich reference list of readings to follow up with.

It's clear that both authors have a wealth of knowledge that they can draw up. They come from different walks of life, have a wide range of experiences and are experts in their respective fields of negotiation and entrepreneurship. It's also clear that the authors want readers to think entrepreneurially, establish entrepreneurial ventures, maximize the benefits and generate value for all stakeholders through effective negotiation skills in the short and long terms. Entrepreneurial negotiation is well understood by the authors due to their long-term, close relationships with thousands of entrepreneurs all over the world, as well as their extensive research, collaborative projects, training and consulting. Readers also stand to gain a great deal from the book's rich and lucid writing.

In sum, I have no hesitation in stating that this book is a must-read for all prospective entrepreneurs: serial entrepreneurs, women entrepreneurs, minority entrepreneurs, ethnic entrepreneurs, youth entrepreneurs, student entrepreneurs, mid-career and established entrepreneurs alike.

Jaideep Prabhu, PhD
Professor of Marketing
Jawaharlal Nehru Professor of Indian Business & Enterprise
Director of the *Centre for India & Global Business (CIGB)*
Fellow of Clare College
Cambridge Judge Business School
University of Cambridge, UK

PREFACE

In the twenty-first century, the world has witnessed an unprecedented surge in the acceptability of entrepreneurship as a career. It is getting widely popular as a career option for youngsters and middle-aged people to solve societal problems and add significant value to the customers' experience. Right from an idea to the execution and growth of an enterprise, entrepreneurship entails several steps and processes leading to the desired outcomes. Thus, it calls for unique skillsets by entrepreneurs. However, in each phase of entrepreneurship—from idea to the opportunity, from the opportunity to the business plan, from the business plan to funding the venture, from funding the venture to launching, growing and ending the venture—the entrepreneur needs to connect, communicate and empathize with the counterpart to set up, run and grow the entrepreneurial venture.

Specially, as mentioned, communication has a very crucial role to play in the entrepreneurial success of any venture. The important aspects of communication, such as, influence, persuasion and ability to convince others, are highly essential. The structured and polished approach to understand and apply such an advanced communication skill is recognized as negotiation. Thus, the art of negotiation is pivotal to the success of any entrepreneurial venture.

The book encompasses the entrepreneurs' specific issues, dilemmas and complex situations in the VUCA environment. Various types and levels of negotiations are conducted between the parties involved to safeguard the mutual interests, goals and long-term relationships. Right from the beginning of startup idea to the exit of the venture involves several negotiation-based planning, strategies, tactics and description of cases in relation to competitors, suppliers, creditors, distributors, wholesalers, retailers, customers, government entities, civil societies, regulatory systems, international agencies and so on. Such varied forms of negotiation led to the venture creation, growth, expansion, diversification and, eventually, the successful exit of the venture in the longer run.

Negotiation skills are a universal requirement. However, the nature of problems differs for the entrepreneurs, unlike senior executives with limited authority and confined area of operations. Entrepreneurs are the highest risk takers in any business context. They are the ones who are going to lose entirely if the entrepreneurial venture fails. Besides, risk factor, they need to be innovators and carry multiple cognitive and non-cognitive skills to gauge the complex situations and opportunities as they arrive. They need to envision the blue ocean and be the first mover. They need to be intuitive and carry forward-thinking abilities to grab unforeseen opportunities in the market. These efforts and initiatives require them to be equipped with specific skills such as negotiation. It is to protect the best interests of both the parties or partners in the deal-making process. Even though negotiation styles and tactics may remain universal, however, the contextual difference, issues, nature of discussion, high-risk presence, types of stakeholders involved and so on make entrepreneurs inevitable to have the effective negotiation skills to sail through.

The general books on negotiation available to entrepreneurs do not address specific issues, challenges, situations and case scenarios. These unique contexts are exclusively confronted and experienced by the entrepreneurs at different phases of entrepreneurship.

Against the backdrop of entrepreneurship, the central objective of our book is to equip entrepreneurs with an essential modern-day skill of negotiation with all stakeholders in venture creation and development.

INTRODUCTION

The authors penned down the present textbook, with a clear purpose to guide, motivate and encourage readers from a different background who aim to pursue their entrepreneurial dreams by employing effective negotiation skills. It offers the readers a unique experience of learning through a variety of chapters intersecting the areas of negotiation and entrepreneurship. All the topics presented in chapters have been meticulously curated keeping in view the impact and benefits to the readers. The textbook consists of ten chapters ranging from introduction to entrepreneurship, interpersonal behavior, role of communication, conflict management, negotiation planning and strategy, negotiation process and effective tips, negotiation for women, negotiation and cultural differences.

Chapter 1 provides an overview of entrepreneurship and the entrepreneur's role in society. Entrepreneurship has always been a component of our traditional cultures and old civilizations in general, even from the beginning of recorded history. Understanding entrepreneurship from an entirely new angle is extremely important in today's competitive business environment. The dynamic changes in the internal and external environment of business necessitate a new perspective and a deeper understanding of the available data.

When it comes to starting a venture and dealing with conflicts, Chapter 2 is all about it. All of the things that stand in the way of starting your own enterprise lead to conflict. Entrepreneurs must learn how to deal with a variety of competing situations while preserving relationships rather than tearing them apart. Entrepreneurs can learn about various conflict resolution strategies, models and styles by studying various approaches to a conflict. As an entrepreneur, conflict management is one of the most sought-after abilities. When dealing with a variety of scenarios including opposing viewpoints and competing interests, these abilities are critical.

According to Chapter 3, entrepreneurs need to communicate well in order to succeed. Successful entrepreneurs have the ability to articulate their thoughts and feelings as well as their problem-solving abilities through

xxii   NEGOTIATION FOR ENTREPRENEURSHIP

effective communication. It also fosters trust, openness and transparency. An entrepreneur's ability to successfully manage any problem rests on their ability to communicate at many levels, as well as their use of various techniques and methods. It's a skill that any entrepreneur should be able to master and put to use in a variety of business management scenarios. It aids the entrepreneur in establishing trusting relationships with other members of the entrepreneurship community.

Chapter 4 covers the interpersonal dynamics of an entrepreneur. Entrepreneurial success in any industry is heavily influenced by the individual characteristics of the entrepreneur. An entrepreneur's unique personal attributes are essential to the success of an enterprise's objectives, goals and vision. It is necessary to gain a deeper knowledge of the mind of an entrepreneur. Based on the dynamics of interpersonal and intrapersonal relationships between individuals, an entrepreneur must be able to gauge the behavior of others or groups of people.

Chapter 5 deals with negotiation for startup ventures. Entrepreneurs rely on the goodwill of the other side in negotiations for the success of their fledgling businesses. Stakeholders might include anyone from coworkers and customers to investors and investors-to-be. There are historical examples of negotiations resulting in agreements that put an end to conflicts. Instead of peace agreements, there exist contracts in the business world, such as those for new ventures.

Chapter 6 introduces the readers to the key considerations an entrepreneur must pay attention to while striking a negotiation-based deal with their counterparts. When starting a venture, entrepreneurs often have low resources and weak negotiating strength, yet in order to grow their business, they must engage in multiple negotiations. A company may engage in such negotiations with a possible employee or a potential lender as well as with potential customers. Entrepreneurs need to learn the fundamentals of negotiating in order to get the best results for themselves.

In Chapter 7, the ten most important laws of negotiation are discussed in detail. Each and every entrepreneur will have to deal with negotiations at some point in their professional lives. The problem is that many entrepreneurs are unaware that negotiations are a multistep process that is dependent on the selection of the most appropriate strategy. The laws of negotiation help the readers become knowledgeable and proactive in entrepreneurial decisions with their counterparts.

In this Chapter 8, the authors provide some of the more creative approaches that women entrepreneurs might take to negotiating in order to get the best possible results for themselves and the other parties involved. Winning in negotiations means offering your counterparts a range of options, and this is especially true for women business owners. When women entrepreneurs create alternatives for their counterparts, they show that they are concerned about their needs as well as their own financial gain.

Female entrepreneurs are less successful than their male counterparts when it comes to starting their own businesses. The primary cause of this phenomenon can be traced back to cultural differences. Women in different cultures are expected to meet different standards. The breadwinning tasks like entrepreneurship are traditionally reserved for men in various countries, where women are supposed to take care of home duties. As a result of this, women are still taking up entrepreneurial roles in order to provide financial support for their families when their male spouses aren't. There is a big difference between starting a business and making it successful. Chapter 9 focuses on the challenges that women experience while starting their own businesses and how they might overcome them.

Chapter 10 includes negotiation in the context of culture. Negotiations are complicated by cultural differences. Entrepreneurs need to be aware of the importance of cultural differences when conducting business around the world. When developing cross-cultural negotiation methods, entrepreneurs can benefit from having a firm grasp of cultural nuances. When negotiating, they must be mindful of their own culture and how it differs from the culture of their business partners. The level of individualism vs. collectivism varies widely between cultures. Businesses must remember that people negotiate in different ways, such as the direct approach taken by negotiators in individualistic cultures and the indirect approach taken by those in collective cultures. The self-serving bias of fairness is vital for entrepreneurs from cultures that emphasize individualism.

As a whole, the chapters offer a wealth of information, insights and distinct perspectives through the use of several case scenarios and examples. In the context of entrepreneurship, it would assist the readers to understand the complexities and subtleties of the negotiation process more clearly. Entrepreneurs will be better equipped to achieve effective outcomes as a result of reading this textbook, which provide a complete understanding of all areas of entrepreneurial negotiation.

PART I

ENTREPRENEURSHIP IN THE TWENTY-FIRST CENTURY: MANAGING IN A VUCA WORLD

Chapter 1

ENTREPRENEURSHIP AND THE ENTREPRENEUR

Learning Objectives

1. To understand the concept of entrepreneurship
2. To highlight the factors responsible for the wider acceptance of entrepreneurship in the twenty-first century
3. To appreciate some prominent entrepreneurs and their entrepreneurial contributions
4. Learn about entrepreneurial intention and the resulting entrepreneurial ventures
5. To introduce sustainability entrepreneurship that solves societal issues

OPENING PROFILE: NEGOTIATING WITH WALMART BUYERS

Walmart buyers are trained to treat their vendors in a variety of ways, depending on where the vendor fits into their plan. This case shares the story of a vendor called Sarah who negotiated a win-win outcome with Walmart. Walmart, the world's largest retailer, sold $514.4 billion worth of goods in 2019. Partnerships can be seen as either the Holy Grail or the kiss of death, given the firm's laser-like concentration on EDLP (everyday low pricing) and its ability to make or break suppliers.

Sarah Talley (owner of Frey Farms) acquired a deep understanding of the Walmart culture while finding "new money" in the supply chain through innovative tactics. For example, Frey Farms used school buses ($1,500 each) instead of tractors ($12,000 each) as a cheaper and faster way to transport melons to the warehouse.

Talley also was skillful at negotiating a coveted co-management supplier agreement with Walmart, showing how Frey Farms could share the responsibility of managing inventory levels and sales and ultimately save customer's money while improving their own margins.

> When you have a problem, when there's something you engage in with Walmart that requires agreement so that it becomes a negation, the first advice is to think in partnership teams, really focus on a common goal, for example, getting costs out and ask questions. Do not make demands or statements. Rather ask if you can do this better. If the relationship with Walmart is truly a partnership, negating to resolve differences should focus on long-term mutual partnership gains.
>
> Do not spend time gripping. Be a problem solver instead. Approach Walmart by saying, "Let's work together and drive cost down and produce it so much cheaper you do not have to replace me because if you work with me I could do it better."

What Is Entrepreneurship?

Today, entrepreneurship has become one of the most sought-after paths for people of all ages. To understand the entrepreneurship in today's VUCA environment can be subject to a short life cycle. VUCA is an abbreviated term and means volatility, uncertainty, complexity and ambiguity and is witnessed in the business environment all over the world. These four factors play a significant role in deciding how businesses operate in each business environment. A key factor of this environment is the entrepreneur. Being an entrepreneur, one needs to assemble all the essential resources and work with people who possess different capabilities. This enables the entrepreneurs to succeed in establishing, scaling and sustaining the entrepreneurial venture. Fundamentally, the entrepreneur solves the social and economic problems faced by customer segments in different markets. These solutions are driven by entrepreneurial creativity and innovation that aid in solving the problems of the customer by offering quality products or services in a cost-effective manner.

In simple terms, entrepreneurship is a process to start and run a new entrepreneurial venture, carrying an innovative idea or seizing an opportunity to solve the pain points of customers by offering products, services and technological solutions, thus leading to commercial gains. Besides, entrepreneurship assumes risks and rewards associated with it as a motivating factor. Differently stated, entrepreneurship is a mind-set to change the status quo and add value to the existing environment by seeking innovative solutions. It is the creative mind-set of an individual who solves the problem innovatively, with limited resources and constraints. Risk involvement and immense opportunity to scale up the entrepreneurial venture in the future are also the motivating factors for an entrepreneur to start the entrepreneurial venture.

Entrepreneurship is the process of creating something new with value by devoting the necessary time and effort to assume the accompanying financials, psychic, social risk and uncertainties with rewards of monetary and personal satisfaction. (Definitions of entrepreneurship, Refer Table 1.1.)

In the early stages of entrepreneurship research, the primary focus was on the individual characteristics and personality traits of entrepreneurs. The focus was mostly on small enterprises (Diffey, 1982; Hisrich & O'Brien, 1982). The challenge in the initial years, to recognize entrepreneurship as a field of knowledge, required significant contributions from practitioners and scholars in entrepreneurship. However, the contributions made centered on theoretical exploration and causality relationships (Hisrich et al., 2010).

Similarly, it is interesting to understand the entrepreneurial process of the entrepreneur. In the entrepreneurial process, the entrepreneur enjoys the flexibility and diversity present in the entrepreneurial venture. Flexibility is understood in terms of owning the innovation venture and making major decisions in the interest of the organization. As an entrepreneur, having the flexibility to make the decision for the entrepreneurial venture is one of the critical aspects of entrepreneurship.

Like flexibility, diversity provides advantages for an entrepreneurial venture. Diversity is understood in terms of creative ideas, market opportunities and unsolved pain points of customers. It drives the entrepreneur to take calculated risk and apply entrepreneurial skills by starting and scaling up the venture.

Another important aspect of entrepreneurship is innovation. Innovation is a continuous and cyclical process. Innovation involves different stages starting from converting a basic idea into a real solution to the customer's problem (Damanpour, 1991; Poole & Vande Ven, 1989). However, when innovation is defined as an outcome, it becomes a tangible product, service or knowledge creation for the greater good (Ford, 1996).

The modern perspective of entrepreneurship is changing. The new generation visualizes the problems and challenges of society from a different perspective. Today, the young generation wants to be independent, in terms of making decisions and managing one's own career and life. They prefer less interference in their own activities. We also see the changing mind-set of the Millennials while they acquire skills, knowledge and expertise in the universities, vocational centers, business centers and other centers of excellence. These learning centers, universities, vocational centers, business schools, research and development centers are now including entrepreneurship as a regular course and/or a full-time program for the aspiring student entrepreneurs. Structured curriculum and innovative pedagogical tools have been developed to meet the standard and requirements of the student. The core focus is to educate and train the new generation and equip them with the entrepreneurial skills while motivating them to establish and manage innovative entrepreneurial ventures.

Table 1.1 Definitions of entrepreneurship.

Source	Definition
Stevenson and Gumpert (1985)	Entrepreneurship is all about chasing the opportunities in a given situation of resource constraints.
Shane and Venkatraman (2001)	Finding the opportunity in the first place is the key. Concern for limited resources and managing them arises at a later stage in entrepreneurship. The founder gets influenced by the past industry experience, and choices are made.
Shane and Venkatraman (2001)	Entrepreneurship is an area in business. It helps the entrepreneur to understand, exploit the opportunity and convert it into something new in terms of products or services.
Kuratko and Hodgetts (2004)	Entrepreneurship has been understood as a dynamic process. It entails vision, goal, objective and creation.
Allen (2006)	Entrepreneurship is a mind-set of an individual. It looks for opportunities. It seeks innovative ways to grow. Big companies encourage such a mind-set to initiate and challenge the status quo and bring a change toward a positive direction.

Why Is Entrepreneurship So Important in the Twenty-First Century?

Our future has immense possibilities. However, these immense possibilities cannot be visualized by most. Most tend to ignore them when they occur. How we view these possibilities directs how we explore the area further. Being futuristic helps an individual to plan and strategize. It helps us to understand the challenges we may encounter and to visualize our goals and objectives at an early stage. Compared to the past, more than ever before, entrepreneurial opportunities have been increasing around the world; also an entrepreneurial ecosystem is being cultivated by international agencies and government bodies in both entrepreneurial developed and developing economies. A few decades ago, we would infrequently have the opportunity to put entrepreneurial efforts in the right direction due to the absence of proper guidance, expertise and financial support from other serial entrepreneurs, angel investors, venture capitalist and government funding organizations. The entrepreneurial ecosystem was not cultivated due to inadequate and ineffective policy measures. The entrepreneurs would feel isolated and was harder to begin the entrepreneurial journey. The amount of risk involved in the venture makes the aspiring entrepreneur very concerned.

To assess the opportunities, it is necessary to comprehend the trends in business, industry and the economy; understanding these trends helps the entrepreneur to understand the expectation of the market and learn the customer sentiments. For instance, previously infographics was quite popular. Those who were following the industry trends grabbed the opportunity and entered infographics marketing. Usually, entrepreneurs think in the short term and have problems, for trivial reasons, to move ahead and instead lose the opportunity.

Another activity that is important in being a successful entrepreneur is the concept of giving back. This could take the form of giving back to the university, the community, or some other purpose such as individuals in need. An example of the latter occurred in New York State during the quarantine. This is discussed in Table 1.2.

The twenty-first century has seen significant technological disruptions. Unlike sustainable innovation, disruptive innovation-led new entrepreneurial ventures are being established in large numbers in the twenty-first century. Disruption is a process that helps the entrepreneurs and small and medium-size enterprises (SMEs) challenge larger businesses despite limited resources. The new trend of disruptive innovation has been around for the last two decades. For instance, Airbnb is a good example of disruptive innovation. The company started in 2008 disrupting the entire hotel industry worldwide with its unique business model and other processes. Another major trend is the usage of the entrepreneurial ventures driven by disruptive technology. Netflix, Spotify and Roadrunner Recycling are some of the entrepreneurial ventures driven by disruption technology. These entrepreneurial ventures are growing exponentially since their inception.

More and more enterprises are realizing the importance of remote work culture. Telecommuting and online projects are the new work formats in the twenty-first century as it helps the enterprise to reduce the leasing and transportation costs and assists in hiring the most talented individuals around the world. Employees feel good about change which allows them to avoid long traveling hours to the office and hectic schedules. However, remote work has its own problems. Still, trends of remote work, remote teams and remote platforms have become increasingly the new norm of the twenty-first century.

Another growing trend is interactive marketing for entrepreneurs and SMEs. Twitter is a good example of interactive marketing using social media which enables users to comment and retweet about the advertisements shown. Twitter effectively serves the customer through interactive marketing of communication, unlike most traditional marketing. Entrepreneurs in the twenty-first century cannot afford to ignore such emerging trends that are affecting the enterprises, operations and bottom line.

There are several other modern trends, such as automation and the Internet of Things, that have impacted all types of businesses around the

Table 1.2 How a direct-to-consumer shirt brand is giving back?

When New York State went into quarantine, partners Jeffrey Costello and Robert
Tagliapietra had moved their direct-to-consumer shirt company, JCRT, to a
new office on Pier 59 in NYC. JCRT, founded in 2016, commemorates plaid and
camouflage items that have colorful patterns which they name after rock stars and
movies.

Quarantined to their rental home in rural New Jersey, Costello and Tagliapietra
decided to work. New York City, their base and home for years, was the epicenter
of the Covid-19 outbreak. They decided to help friends on the frontlines by sewing
masks using sample fabrics. Tagliapietra boxed hundreds and sent them to wherever
they heard PPE was needed.

"Everything was sort of unknown at that point," Tagliapietra says. "We were very
happy to be able to even do that."

After sewing about 600 masks, their factory in the Dominican Republic reopen after
being closed for quarantine, and they began producing masks for sale and donating;
reaching over 12,000 first responders. They donated a portion of their retail sales
to the New York City Covid-19 Emergency Relief Fund which benefits health care
workers, small businesses and vulnerable workers and families. The marketing effort
was nothing more than their social media posts; they both estimate they have sold
45,000 masks through JCRT and raised more than $65,000 in cash.

Currently selling masks and collared shirts made from a black, red and green plaid with
proceeds go to the Movement for Black Lives. Over Father's Day weekend and the
commemoration of Juneteenth, Costello and Tagliapietra donated 100 percent of
their sales to the Movement for Black Lives and commented "The JCRT community
is pretty responsive."

JCRT is a second entrepreneurship for Costello and Tagliapietra. Together, they
previously founded a women's wear business called Costello Tagliapietra in 2005.
Their runway shows were written up fashion magazines. The founders received a
lot of press for their plaid-on-plaid aesthetics and impressive beards. They were then
labeled "the lumberjacks of fashion."

The women's wear brand struck partnerships with Uniqlo and Kiehl's and was
named twice as a finalist to the CFDA/Vogue Fashion Fund. Their success should
have been eminent but it was not. "We launched right before the big recession,"
Tagliapietra says. "We were never a huge company. We struggled with business and
every single aspect of it."

Upon exiting their first company, Costello and Tagliapietra decided JCRT would be
digital, DTC and greener. "A made to order business model," Tagliapietra explains
"allows us to be a sustainable brand. Our global footprint is as close to zero. We don't
have bolts of fabric or styles to be sold for nothing."

By remaining a small operation, the founders were able to decide where and how to
focus their energies and which causes they support. With their factory running,
JCRT continues to release new designs, selling dress shirts, pants, jackets, bags and
accessories through their website. "This brand is just Jeffrey and I. We can do as we
wish," Tagliapietra says.

Source: https://www.inc.com/matt-haber/jcrt-fashion-direct-to-consumer-masks-black-lives-matter
-pride.html

world. Automation, a big trend in recent decades, is being used more and more in systems and processes. Robots, autonomous vehicles, cognitive agents, household appliances, robo advisors and robotic processes are some of the uniquely designed automation-driven services. The Internet of Things is a revolution in the twenty-first century. It has created new business models and can provide real-time information on critical systems. It can also provide global visibility of different processes besides offering the option of revenue generation. With the help of the Internet of Things, wearable gadgets, such as smart watches and glasses, are being used to better connect individuals globally.

The above-mentioned trends and conditions have provided significant market opportunities for entrepreneurs to start their own entrepreneurial ventures in the twenty-first century. It is a new revolutionary change capable of introducing a paradigm shift in the areas of entrepreneurship and innovation. Along with the availability of new technological advancements and disruptive innovation, entrepreneurs now have an even more fertile ground to think innovatively and unconventional on novel trends making it easier for the entrepreneurs to understand the unmet customer's needs, engage in customization or personalization and better serve the customer.

Prominent Example Entrepreneurs

Entrepreneurship is predominantly driven by passion and curiosity. The capability of the entrepreneur to envision the future makes a bigger difference. It is not a skill that can be acquired just through formal training. Entrepreneurship skills are nurtured by putting oneself in a different circumstance. Undergoing the different stages of entrepreneurial learning enables the entrepreneur to unlearn, lose, win and relearn from a fresh perspective. An entrepreneur acquires entrepreneurial skills when one dares to dream big and think innovatively. Entrepreneurial efforts start by solving the problems of the customers and bridge the opportunity gaps in the market.

One of the prominent entrepreneurs of the twenty-first century is Elon Musk, the cofounder of the electronic payment firm, PayPal. Previously to PayPal he formed the spacecraft company, Space X, and was CEO of the electronic car manufacture, Tesla. Musk is widely considered to be an entrepreneur who is willing to take high risk. All his unconventional entrepreneurial ventures have been initially set up with a substantial risk of failure. In the initial stages of these entrepreneurial ventures, he faced a lot of rejections and discouragements. There were not many like-minded people available to trust his entrepreneurship skills, intuitiveness and support his entrepreneurial ideas, plans and strategies.

Jan Cameron is another prominent entrepreneur who founded Kathmandu clothing company of which she lately sold 51 percent share of the company for 247 million Australian dollars. She is one of the richest women in Australia and runs various companies around the world. Her business interest included: a baby-food company, Bellamy organics and Van Diemen's Land Company Dairy. She also has ownership in several companies, such as Pumpkin Patch, Macpac, Postie Plus Group, Arbuckles Manchester Chain and Dog's Breakfast Furniture Company. Jan Cameron, like many entrepreneurs, is not ready to thrive with one or two ventures. Rather, they set up several companies with unique ideas to solve customers' problems. Richard Branson of Virgin Group is also a good example.

Travis Kalanick is one such entrepreneur who is best known for his revolutionary entrepreneurial venture Uber—a global transportation company. In addition, he is the founder of Scour, a popular peer-to-peer file sharing application, and Red Swoosh, a peer-to-peer content delivery network.

Gary Vaynerchuk is an entrepreneur who runs different entrepreneurial ventures around the world. He is a Belarusian-American entrepreneur who initially cofounded Resy and Empathy Wines, based on his traditional family-run business of wine and creating interest in the digital and social media marketing arena. He is chairman of the board of the communication company VaynerX and is also a best-selling author, prominent speaker and angel-investor as well. Another good example is Tony Hsieh who is an American internet entrepreneur and a venture capitalist. He is best known for the online shoe and clothing company, Zappos. Tony Hsieh began his entrepreneurial venture, LinkExchange, an internet advertising network, which was acquired by Microsoft in 1998 for $265 million each. These entrepreneurs challenged the status quo as each ventured and succeeded in their varied businesses.

In addition, each of these entrepreneurs had different backgrounds, management styles and approaches. They entered into multiple businesses and impacted the industry with their outstanding ideas and business solutions. Each of them had more than one area of expertise and started by establishing one venture. Gradually, they expanded their businesses to unchartered territories and eventually won. Their efforts and contributions started being recognized by the wider communities around the world. These entrepreneurs thrived and sustained for long periods of time in the entrepreneurial ecosystem.

Intentions behind Entrepreneurial Efforts

Each and every entrepreneur has strong intentions to establish their own ventures. Entrepreneurial intentions have been found to use similar conceptions, such as career orientation, nascent entrepreneurs, mental orientation and mind-set. Past research has confirmed that individual entrepreneurial intentions cannot be called common personality traits as there are no uniform conditions, and the entrepreneurial intentions are also difficult to be identified and measured (Shook et al., 2003).

Intentions of an individual can be understood as a purpose or aim to achieve something in the future. It usually is a burning desire that needs to be fulfilled. It can also be a strong reason to address a major concern in one's personal or professional life. As an entrepreneur, intention can be varied. Every entrepreneur is driven by one or more intentions in his/her entrepreneurial ventures Moriano et al. (2012) think of entrepreneurial intention as a conscious state of mind of an entrepreneur that directs entrepreneurial behaviors, such as confronting challenges, fears, dilemmas, bearing risks, collaborating with teams, generating novel ideas, identifying opportunities and starting entrepreneurial ventures.

An interesting study conducted by Oazralli and Rivenburg (2016) focused on the entrepreneurial behavior of United States and Turkish students. The authors studied the antecedents of entrepreneurial behavior by identifying them as social, personality and societal factors. The findings revealed that United States and Turkey students had a positive attitude toward entrepreneurship. However, their entrepreneurial intentions were found to be low. US students showed a higher level of risk attached to starting an entrepreneurial venture. Further, the entrepreneurial intention of Turkish students was to address the economic and political conditions of their home country using entrepreneurship, and they also wanted better educational support, training and resources for entrepreneurship.

The working paper titled "Personality Traits of Entrepreneurs: A Review of Recent Literature" (Kerr et al., 2017) reviewed extensive literature pertaining to the personality traits of entrepreneurs. The review indicated that there were many common results. However, many disagreements were also witnessed among the authors regarding the personality traits of the entrepreneur.

Research indicates that the individuals' personality factors such as strong achievement orientation, risk-taking behavior, perseverance and intelligence have a significant impact on play in entrepreneurial intentions of an entrepreneur (Shaver, 1995). The competent entrepreneur has also been identified as a determining factor in the initial years of an entrepreneurial venture (Garzón, 2010). Some researches posit family background and social environmental factors as influencing entrepreneurial intentions. Some authors found that social environmental factors act as adjusting variable and influence the individual and psychological factors, which lead to the formation of entrepreneurial intentions (Shapero & Sokol, 1982).

Thompson (2009) attempted to bring conceptual clarity on entrepreneurial intentions through his work on entrepreneurial intention and measurement metrics. The research defined entrepreneurial intentions as a strong individual conviction about what they intend to achieve such as setting up a new entrepreneurial venture and, consciously and gradually, working toward realizing it at a definite stage in the future (Thompson, 2009). Research indicates that it is important for the entrepreneur to clearly understand his/her own entrepreneurial intentions to start a new business venture. Each intention must be separately understood under different environmental conditions. An individual must be completely convinced before making the intention to plan and start the entrepreneurial venture.

Sustainability and Entrepreneurship

In recent years, entrepreneurship grabbed attention in the area of sustainability. As a growing field, entrepreneurship has been active in addressing societal and environmental issues. Essentially, the major concerns are increasing deaths due to starvation and malnourishment (e.g., Dean & McMull, 2007; Porter & Kramer, 2011). Social elements, such as women empowerment, gender disparity, differently abled (Mair & Marti, 2006), initiatives for utilization of scarce resources for future consumption, securing future generation (e.g., Cohen & Winn, 2007; Dean & McMullen, 2007) and threats due to global warming, increasing effects of climate change and carbon footprints (e.g., Koegh & Polonsky, 1998) are the major widespread issues that are seeking the attention of entrepreneurs to resolve these issues from the bottom up.

Sustainability and entrepreneurship initiatives have a common goal to serve the community and society at large. The aim is to secure earth through better ecological and environmental practices and approaches, in turn, supporting human beings and the sustenance of flora and fauna across the globe. Some sustainable initiatives through entrepreneurial efforts are being undertaken recently. Since these smaller initiatives often remain stand-alone and fragmented activities, the anticipated outcomes face delay. The gradual constant impact on environmental sustainability will enable entrepreneurship to change the landscape of holistic development.

Sustainability entrepreneurship is indeed gaining prominence over the last few years. The objective is to solve social and environmental problems being faced. Sustainability entrepreneurship is increasingly visible in emerging markets in Asia and South-East Asian countries. Sustainable business models are being innovated by global organizations with the support of local communities through the co-creation model. Low carbon business models, green business and social business are the newly coined terms expressing sustainability entrepreneurship. Under the ambit of sustainable practices, entrepreneurial effort is a common but major factor that helps sustainable development measures to become effective in impacting the larger community.

Sustainable entrepreneurship-led practice acts as an interface between politics, business, law and civil societies, uniting them for larger ecological friends. In practice, sustainable business models implemented in emerging markets such as India, Brazil, China, Indonesia and Philippines positively impact the low-income buyers. However, regional economies of these countries have their own problems and issues. It is important for the entrepreneur to consider the grassroots-level issues while they plan their entrepreneurial ventures. The entrepreneur pays attention to innovative practices and should meet the requirements of internal organizational activities. However, the entrepreneur must also pay attention to sustainable and innovative business models for the growth, expansion and diversification of the entrepreneurial venture. This encourages innovative processes, practices and culture to evolve over a period of time leading to sustainable entrepreneurship.

One example of this is Nest Learning Thermostat. Unlike conventional and programmable thermostats, Nest Learning Thermostat is quite simple to use and conserve energy. The sustainable and innovative product has been manufactured by Nest Lab in Silicon Valley, California, United States. The key feature of the innovative thermostat is that the device is technologically developed to learn from household behavior. Automatically, the thermostat gets used to household routines, preferences and patterns. It works to adjust the high or low temperatures. The device works well according to household members by adjusting the temperature based on the number of members who go out or come in. Within a week's time of installation, the innovative thermostat functions to turn down the heating system in the absence of members at home. Aligning entrepreneurship with sustainability enables the entrepreneur to look for innovative solutions which need to be mindful of all entrepreneurial actions and include sustainability measures as part of the entrepreneurial process and venture creation-cum-development.

Chapter Summary

The chapter summarizes the concept of entrepreneurship and the role of the entrepreneur. Since time immemorial, entrepreneurship has been a part of our traditional cultures and ancient civilizations at large. However, in today's socioeconomic environment, understanding entrepreneurship from a fresh perspective is quite relevant. Several environmental factors, such as the advancement of technology, disruptive innovation, migration of population, climate change, alarming healthcare facilities, market opportunities shifting to emerging markets, shrining and erratic economies, customers' high expectations and demands have influenced the way businesses operate. This calls for a fresh outlook and insight through data analysis.

An entrepreneur never engages in entrepreneurial ventures solely for the sake of wealth accumulation. For sure, financial well-being is important for any business venture at each stage of growth. Yet, wealth creation and accumulation can never be the sole purpose of an entrepreneurial venture. Successful entrepreneurs acknowledge that the strong motivating factors for their entrepreneurial ventures are curiosity, passion, achievement of one's dream, solving the problems of another, introducing innovative products/services, identifying and grabbing the right opportunity, generating employment, supporting the economy and providing financial assistance to support the entrepreneurial ecosystem for future entrepreneurs. Most importantly, it is the sense of autonomy and ownership which get the entrepreneur excited about one's entrepreneurial venture.

Speed, accuracy, agility, creativity, breakthrough innovation, cutting-edge technologies, emerging business models, cost-effective products/service, innovative supply chain and logistics arrangements, automation and operational efficiency, entrepreneurial leadership, employer–employee relationship, work from home culture and virtual teams are some of the prominent core characteristics of the twenty-first century that demand novel approaches, best practices and sustainable solutions affecting different income groups and groups of people around the world. To meet the high expectation of all stakeholders, entrepreneurship rises to the occasion and acts as a linchpin to integrate and synchronize social fabrics, business structures, people, technology, processes and systems. It helps to enable and establish self-sustaining communities and societies. Sustainable entrepreneurship needs to be adopted and nurtured by the developing and developed nations around the globe, transforming and sustaining all aspects of societies.

Key Terms

- Entrepreneurial intensions
- Entrepreneurs
- Entrepreneurship
- Sustainability
- VUCA environments

Review Questions

Q.1 Discuss the role of entrepreneurship in modern times. List the advantages of promoting the culture of entrepreneurship in schools, colleges and universities.

Q.2 Select your own list of most admired entrepreneurs in the twenty-first century. Name the entrepreneurial ventures and state the reasons.

Q.3 Identify any four major challenges faced by either a developed or developing nation due to the VUCA environment.

Q.4 What do you understand by entrepreneurial intentions? How important is it for an entrepreneur to start an entrepreneurial venture? Support with arguments.

Q.5 How do you think sustainability issues can be strongly addressed by entrepreneurship? Discuss.

Q.6 Select your own list of two entrepreneurial ventures and elaborate on the key opportunities seized by the entrepreneur.

YOU BE THE ENTREPRENEUR

Donald Katz is a well-known personality in the entertainment and educational programming arena since early 2000. He is known for his entrepreneurial venture by the name *Audible*. The company is the largest seller of downloadable audiobooks. Audible was started in 1995. By 2016, users almost downloaded two billion hours of content. However, the company has now been sold to Amazon. The growth story of Katz is incredible. The life of Katz was not always the path of roses as he narrates his story, his background and his work experience. This helps one to know how he started the world's first spoken-audio entertainment on the internet.

The company provides "all-at-one-place" offerings, so the approach acts as a unique selling proposition for the company. The concept is unique as readers can read a variety of books and find it exciting to visit the company's website to explore the types of available audiobooks. More reluctant readers, those who find it difficult to read books for longer periods of time, also get attracted to the Audible company's audiobooks. These audiobooks are available in different languages and on a variety of subjects.

Audible derives its revenue through monthly subscriptions. The reader pays $8 per book or $16 for two books a month. One can also purchase the books for about $16–$20. The customer segment of the company is the Millennials. About 48 percent of users have been found to be below the age of 35. The key partners of the company are a large number of book publishers. Over the years, Audible has set its terms so well that the company has become a dominant platform for book publishers. The cost structure has also been well managed by the company. Payments to authors, royalties to book publishers, other expenses, platform maintenance costs and marketing costs are the major part of the cost structure of the company. Affiliate marketing in recent years has helped the company reach different customer segments.

In the early years of his career, Katz worked with *Rolling Stone* Magazine as a correspondent. He covered stories of terrorism, revolution, struggle, independence and rebellion around the world. Katz then switched to his passion—writing. According to him, his vast years of experience as an international correspondent and writer guided him to think with imagination, creativity and novel practices. He admits that the uniqueness or novelty of his thought process is due to his exposure to varied experiences in the past. His curiosity to explore new and unchartered territories played a major role in understanding himself better. It further helped him to explore his entrepreneurial desires and understand the nuances of the situation, people, culture and nations. All this helped him visualize and understand the pulse of his audience and *Audible*, as an entrepreneurial venture was born.

"Many elements that make Audible a distinct company in many ways has a higher purpose drawn upon the many things I experience as a writer," he explains.

Source: 'Pushing the limits' by Priyadarshini Patwa, February 2019 www.centrepreneur.com

CASE SCENARIO

Shan Haider was a language teacher who traveled to different countries between 2010 and 2015 as part of his teaching assignment. He made a subtle observation while he was traveling globally. He realized that the business around the work is facing a particular problem, a shortage of trained workers. Shan saw a great entrepreneurial opportunity waiting for him and started his entrepreneurial journey. He founded the enterprise, Teacherux, an HRtech in Istanbul, Turkey. He later established another office in New York.

Initially, Shan started with the placement of teachers by filling the available position in Instanbul, his native city. Shan found the pace of growth to be slower than expected. In order to capture the huge, untapped opportunity present around the world, Shan scaled the venture by adopting cutting-edge technology enabling the company to match the profiles of teachers with the actual requirements of the schools. Shan relied on a machine learning platform and analytics to accurately match the profiles in geographic locations. Also, the technological support helped him categorize the profiles of teachers according to the social and religious sensitivities.

This unique tech-based service was the USP of Teacherix under SaaS platform. Teachers found the online platform highly beneficial in comparison to other available options. Now teachers could upload their profiles, regularly check the latest job positions and could be contacted easily by the company when their profile fit the requirements. As part of one-time registration, teachers paid the company. If the teacher is not offered the job in the next 120 days, the company refunded the entire deposited amount. Similarly, each school paid $650 initial fee to partner with Teacherix. The company demonstrates transparency, agility and responsiveness toward its client. According to Shan, "Simply put, my company helps schools connect to teachers globally."

The projection for the company is very good. In the next three years, according to Shan, Teacherix will build a business of $100 million in revenue.

The entrepreneurial story of Teacherix shows that an entrepreneur, in spite of inadequate background in technology, can build and scale an enterprise.

Imagine a situation where your international office nominate you to travel for a month to a new city for business development. While living in the new city and meeting new people, you get invited by a local NGO to visit the center for differently abled teenagers and you encourage them with a motivational talk. Assuming that you were looking for an entrepreneurial opportunity, discuss one potential entrepreneurial opportunity which you may like to explore by engaging these differently abled teenagers? Propose a brief plan to move this idea forward.

Source: "Turkish entrepreneur's HRtech startup helps international schools find best teachers" by Vishal Krishna, July 2020. www.yourstory.com

Suggested Reading

1. Entrepreneurship theory, process and practice in the twenty-first century

Kuratko, Donald. (2011). Entrepreneurship, theory, process, and practice in the 21st century. *International Journal of Entrepreneurship and Small Business*, 13, 8–17. 10.1054/ IJESB.2011.040412

This article examines the one true enduring force that fuels a market and economy, that is, entrepreneurship and the innovation it creates. However, the same force surges in the growing field of entrepreneurship education in the midst of this huge expansion of entrepreneurship theory, process and practice. This article reviews all three components and highlights some of the critical questions that confront entrepreneurship education in the twenty-first century and how entrepreneurship educators can be the solution to those questions.

2. Sustainability in entrepreneurship: A tale of two logics

De Clerq, D., & Voronove, M. (2011). Sustainability in entrepreneurship: A tale of two logics. *International Small Business Journal*, 29(4), 322–344.

This article theorizes how the characteristics of the field, as well as entrepreneur characteristics and actions, influence the legitimacy derived from adhering to the field-prescribed balance between sustainability and profitability. Given the uncertainty surrounding the role and meaning of sustainability in business practice, it is important to explore the legitimacy drivers that newcomers (entrepreneurs) to a field derive from balancing sustainability and profitability.

3. Entrepreneurship and development in the twenty-first century

Sergi, B.S. & Scanlon, C.C. (2019). *Entrepreneurship and development in the 21st century* (First Edition). Emerald Publishing Limited.

Spurring the creation of new technologies and new jobs, the role of entrepreneurs now affects globalization and amplifies the dynamics of markets and economic growth. The book addresses entrepreneurship in developed and developing countries; entrepreneurial development and business innovation; the role of entrepreneurial education and contextual and environmental factors in developing entrepreneurial intention and behavior among university graduates; the evolution of financing entrepreneurship; how data can identify and shape consumer behavior in e-commerce; and metrics to understand how people choose to trust reviews which focus on Amazon reviews.

References

Allen, K. (2006). *Launching New Ventures*. Boston: Houghton Mifflin.

Cohen, B., and Winn, M. I. (2007). 'Market imperfections, opportunity and sustainable entrepreneurship'. *Journal of Business Venturing*, Vol. 22, No. 1, pp. 29–49.

Damanpour, F. (1991). 'Organizational innovations: A meta-analysis of effects of determinants and moderators'. *Academy of Management Journal*, Vol. 34, pp. 555–590.

Dean, T.J., and McMullen, J. S. (2007). 'Toward a theory of sustainable entrepreneurship: Reducing environmental degradation through entrepreneurial action'. *Journal of Business Venturing*, Vol. 22, No. 1, pp. 50–76.

Diffley, J. H. (1982). 'A study of woman business owners and the importance of selected entrepreneurial competencies related to educational programs'. *Dissertation Abstracts International*, Vol. 43, p. 1802A.

Ford, C. M. (1996). 'A theory of individual creative action in multiple social domains'. *Academy of Management Review*, Vol. 21, pp. 1112–1142.

Garzón, M. D. (2010). 'A comparison of personal entrepreneurial competences between entrepreneurs and CEOs in service sector'. *Service Business*, Vol. 4, pp. 289–303.

Hisrich, R. D., and O'Brien, M. (1982). 'The woman entrepreneur as a reflection of the type of business'. In K. Vesper (Ed.), *Frontiers of Entrepreneurship Research*, pp. 54–67. Wellesley, MA: Babson College.

Hisrich, Robert D., Peters, Michael, and Shepherd, Dean A. (2010). *Entrepreneurship*, 8th ed. Homewood, IL: McGraw Hill Irwin.

Huhn, T. S. (1962). *The Structure of Scientific Revolutions*. Chicago: University of Chicago Press.

Kerr, S. P., Kerr, W., and Xu, T. (2017, November). 'Personality traits of entrepreneurs: A review of recent literature'. Working Paper No. 18-0470. https://www.hbs.edu/faculty/Publication%20Files/KKX-Personality-Review_RIS_5ea5da25-c8ab-41d2-90ee-e30b3d5b071c.pdf.

Koegh, P. D., and Polonsky, M. J. (1998). 'Environmental commitment: A basis for environmental entrepreneurship?' *Journal of Organizational Change Management*, Vol. II, No. 1, pp. 38–49

Kuratko, D., and Hodgetts, R. (2004). *Entrepreneurship*, 6th ed. Mason, OH: Thompson-Southwestern.

Mair, J., and Marti, L. (2006). 'Social entrepreneurship research: A source of explanation, prediction, and delight'. *Journal of World Business*, Vol. 41, No. 1, pp. 36–44.

Moriano, J. A., Gorgievski, M., Laguan, M,, Stephan, U., and Zarafshani, K. (2012). 'A cross cultural approach to understanding entrepreneurial intention'. *Journal of Career Development*, Vol. 39, No. 2, pp. 162–185.

Ozaralli, N., and Rivenburgh, N. K. (2016). 'Entrepreneurial intentions: Antecedents to entrepreneurial behavior in the U.S.A. and Turkey'. *Journal of Global Entrepreneurship Research*, Vol. 6, p. 3.

Poole, M. S., and Van de Yen, A. H. (1989). 'Toward a general theory of innovation processes'. In A. H. Van de Yen, H. L. Angle, and M. L. Poole (Eds.), *Research on Management of Innovation: The Minnesota Studies*, pp. 637–662. New York: Harper & Row.

Porter, M. E., and Kramer, M. R. (2011). 'Creating shared value'. *Harvard Business Review*, Vol. 89, Nos. 1/2, pp. 62–77.

Scott, S., and Venkataraman, S. (2000). 'The promise of entrepreneurship as a field of research'. *Academy of Management Review*, Vol. 25, pp. 217–226.

Shane, S. A., and Venkataraman, S. (2000). 'The promise of entrepreneurship as a field of research'.

Shane, S., & Venkataraman, S. (2001). Entrepreneurship as a field of research: A response to Zahra and Dess, Singh, and Erikson. *Academy of management review*, Vol. 26, No. 1, pp. 13–16.

Shapero, A., and Sokol, L. (1982). 'The social dimensions of entrepreneurship'. In C. A. Kent, D. L. Sexton, and K. H. Vesper (Eds.), *Encyclopedia of Entrepreneurship*, pp. 72–90. Englewood Cliff, NJ: Prentice-Hall.

Shaver, K. G. (1999). 'The entrepreneurial personality myth'. *Business and Economic Review*, Vol. 41, No. 3, pp. 20–33.

Shook, C. L., Peiwm, R. L., and McGee, J. E. (2003). 'Venture creation and the enterprising individual: A review and synthesis'. *Journal of Management*, Vol. 29, No. 30, pp. 379–399.

Stevenson, H. H., and Gumpert, D. (1985). 'The heart of entrepreneurship'. *Harvard Business Review*, Vol. 85, pp. 85–94.

Stevenson, H. M., and Dial, J. (1995). 'Entrepreneurship: A definition revisited'. *Babson Frontiers of Entrepreneurship Research*, Vol. 15, No. 3, pp. 54–63.

Thompson, E. R. (2009). 'Individual entrepreneurial intent: Construct clarification and development of an internationally reliable metric'. *Entrepreneurship Theory and Practice*, Vol. 33, No. 3, pp. 669–694.

Chapter 2

CONFLICT MANAGEMENT AND ENTREPRENEURSHIP

Learning Objectives

1. To become familiarized with the barriers to entrepreneurship
2. To highlight the major challenges and issues related to conflict
3. To understand the nature and sources of conflict in an entrepreneurial venture
4. To identify the types of conflicts observed in an entrepreneurial venture
5. To highlight approaches to conflict management
6. To learn the ways to manage conflicts in an entrepreneurial venture

OPENING PROFILE: POWER IN CANADIAN TRADE NEGOTIATION

On October 3, 1987, the Free Trade Agreement (FTA) was signed by representatives of Canada and the United States after two strenuous years of intense negotiations. Canada could be described as a medium-sized economy. Its population is one-tenth the size of the United States, which is considered an economic superpower in comparison. More than 75 percent of its exports go to the United States thus making the United States Canada's prime trading partner. By contrast, the United States was exporting less than 20 percent of its products to Canada.

A Royal Commission concluded that Canada's only means to achieve this stability was to engage in an open free trade partnership with the United States. The problem was the United States was not especially interested in such a free trade partnership agreement.

The first step that Canada took was in the form of preparation by developing a succinct plan. A chief negotiator, Simon Reisman, was appointed by the Canadian prime minister himself. He established an ad-hoc organization called the Trade Negotiation Office which reported directly to the Canadian Government Cabinet and had access to the highest levels of bureaucracy. It established in no uncertain terms their negotiation goals and objectives which included a strong dispute resolution mechanism the Canadians felt was vitally important to their success.

In contrast, the United States did not consider the FTA to be especially important and let Canada do all the initial work. The only reason the US Congress even considered the FTA proposal was that they liked the idea of a bilateral approach to trade and were tired of the previous mechanism that failed to settle a host of trade dispute irritants between the two countries known as GATT.

Strong differences in interests and approaches dogged the negotiations. The Canadians used every advantage available including the use of Summit negotiation meeting between the leaders of both countries to emphasize their concerns at every opportunity. Yet, the political powers in the United States dragged their feet to such an extent that the Canadian negotiators walked away from the talks to express their displeasure. This put some heat on the US administrators to the extent that US Treasury Secretary Baker took over the negotiations.

The FTA between the two countries created the largest bilateral trade relationship in the world. Canada achieved its objectives because of its detailed planning and intense focus of its negotiation team despite the asymmetry in power between the two nations.

(This case study shows how a weaker negotiating partner can successfully use power negotiation to win a good agreement with a stronger negotiating partner. There are many occasions when a smaller company will want to form a negotiation partnership with a larger organization to further its business objectives. There are two hurdles that the smaller company might have to overcome to succeed in the negotiation process. The first problem is to get the larger organization's attention as they may express little or no interest in the partnership. The second problem revolves around the prickly issue of negotiating from a much weaker power base. There exists the danger that the smaller party's business goals are not overwhelmed by the more powerful negotiating partner during the negotiating process.)

Barriers to Entrepreneurship

Entrepreneurship as a practice has never been easy. The challenges are significant as the entrepreneurial venture starts and grows. The entrepreneur understands the success of a venture is not attributed to a single factor. There are several factors responsible for the growth and development of an entrepreneurial venture over time. There are usually some barriers to the entrepreneurial process. They affect and deviate the venture from its actual trajectory of economic growth and meeting the customers' demands and high expectations.

Today's entrepreneur is excited about entrepreneurship and its immense possibilities. Through meaningful work, customer value, wealth generation, sustainability plans, job creation, poverty alleviation, healthcare services and technology, the entrepreneur can visualize the positive impacts of these changes in business and society at large. The entrepreneur remains passionate, confident and motivated about the entrepreneurial opportunities. However, many a time, the entrepreneur fails to pay heed to the barriers to fulfilling the entrepreneurial process, identifying and assessing the creative idea and entrepreneurial opportunity, making and executing the business plan, the accessibility to venture funding and the assessment of final performance of the venture. More often than not, the lack of expertise in the initial years of the venture, the cost can be 20 percent more than planned. While the entrepreneur has the tendency to downplay barriers, these barriers threaten the survival and growth of the venture.

Research on the early years of an entrepreneurial venture found these small businesses started generating jobs and impacting the lives of others (Birch, 1979). This and similar observations caused researchers and policy makers to emphasize building an entrepreneurial ecosystem, which led to the formation of an industry association encouraging entrepreneurship. They supported and motivated small firms to think big and contribute to the economic growth of the nation through job creation and higher productivity.

One study, Klapper et al. (2006), focused on the entry regulations for small businesses: expenditures, cost structures, rules and procedures in Europe. The results indicated that the entry regulation had negative effects on small enterprises. Small enterprises were not affected by the regulations related to entry and compliance requirements. Similar results were found in another study (Desai et al., 2003).

Entrepreneurs suffer more when they confront the entrepreneurial barriers due in part to their lack of support and expertise. Several studies identified problems related to barriers faced by entrepreneurs in the initial years. Scarcity of resources, inadequate knowledge about system and management processes, less experience in building a sound business culture, lack of human resource skills to identify talent and build the best team, no insight to find a like-minded cofounder and industry experts and lack of those skills to obtain and manage funds are some of the common problems of entrepreneurs. To deal with all of these, an entrepreneur needs to have the basic resources in place, such as financial, technological, marketing and human resources. Besides planning, the implementation of different management and work processes, such as establishing the right communication channel for the customers, decision-making processes in the teams, selling process to sell and market the products/services to the customer, technological processes to support the overall business strategy, and supply chain and logistics processes for operational efficiency are also important enabling the entrepreneur to manage these resources.

Transition and change have always been a difficult problem, particularly at the start of the first venture. Managing the financial needs of the entrepreneurial venture is one such unexpected work situation where entrepreneurs struggle. Besides obtaining the funds and financial management, the entrepreneur often works long hours to overcome the barriers. This of course negatively affects the work-life balance of the entrepreneur (Lorrain and Laferte, 2006).

Entrepreneurship barriers broadly represent poor entrepreneurial ecosystems, not having smarter people in the team, stiff regulation of market entry and exit, funds crunch and limited resources, "cannot do-it" attitude of the entrepreneur, inadequate entrepreneurial training, guidance and mentoring designed for the entrepreneurs, lack of technical and soft skills, inadequate market and customer experience, fear of failure and risk averseness of the entrepreneur.

However, there are some instances of strong entrepreneurship ecosystems. Entrepreneurship-based support initiatives have been undertaken to build an entrepreneurial mind-set and attitude toward the creation of new entrepreneurial ventures (Boettke and Coyne, 2008). Government schemes related to infrastructure development for venture creation, availability and access to venture funds, building incubation and accelerator centers, collaboration and association with universities and centers of excellence to teach, train and mentor the entrepreneurs and promote entrepreneurship in a digital economy have been undertaken.

One entrepreneur, Kim Perell founder of Perell Ventures' story of dealing with the barriers and fears of starting and growing a venture, is described in Case 2.1

CASE 2.1

Kim Perell, CEO of *Perell Ventures*, can relate to fears that are experienced by entrepreneurs. She explains, "when I started my first company, I had so many what-ifs swirling around in my head. What if my company fails? What if people laugh at me? What if I can't get customers? What if no one believes in me? What if I don't believe in myself?"

Perell's fears became a barrier to starting her own company, and she realized that she would have to acknowledge, address and conquer them. One must take control and identify *fear* as a human emotion that is a barrier to the unknown. Ms Perell shares what she refers to as the five fears all entrepreneurs face (and how to conquer them):

1. **Fear of failure** is frequently a barrier to startup entry among beginning entrepreneurs. In fact, 33 percent of Americans state their fear of failure stops them from starting their own business. Ms Perell states "what must be remembered is failure is not the opposite of success. Failure can be turned around and actually set you up for success." Dyson created 5,126 failed prototypes before finally inventing the bagless vacuum cleaner and worked since 2016 to create an electric vehicle, which would have been a seven-seater with a whopping 600-mile range per charge.

   Failing does not make you a failure; it is giving up that makes a person a failure. In fact, failing can set a person up for success. Studies show that failing in the past makes entrepreneurs more than twice as likely to succeed in the future. Entrepreneurs must ask themselves, "with my potential opportunity; what is the worst-case scenario if I fail?" Then, they must decide if they can live with the worst possible outcome.

2. **Fear of uncertainty** is hard to handle as most individuals tend to default to what is most secure. It may be easier to stay in a dead-end job because you know what to expect day-to-day.

   The fear of the unknown is only unknown until you know it. Take risks and move forward with confidence. For the business to get better there has to be a change, and as long as you are resilient and keep moving forward, you will cultivate, adjust and become more powerful. To help with this fear, remember a time when a life event did not go according to plan. Did you adapt and press forward? How did you succeed?

3. **Fear of rejection** happens to every entrepreneur. But to be a successful entrepreneur, one cannot fear pitching to investors or selling a product/service to customers. After all, the worse that will happen is your pitch may be rejected. That is business! Everyone is faced with rejection. Turning the rejection into a positive will help you because you need the right people to say "yes." When looking for a business partner with deep pockets and confidence in the venture, find someone who is a good fit and the only way to do this is by asking.

   To overcome the barrier of rejection, do not take "no" personally but use it as a learning tool. The more you learn the more on track you will be and soon you will not be receiving a "maybe" or a non-committal "sure" to your pitch.

4. **Fear of not being good enough** means the hardest person to please is "*yourself*." Many entrepreneurs believe they are not good enough to start a business and be successful. Or those who experience success end up feeling as if their success is undeserved. It is difficult to stay positive and confident in the face of uncertainty and setbacks which can be overwhelming when you are questioning your own abilities. Here is Perell's advice:

   • **Invest in relationships.** Find mentors, peers and friends who believe in you and will give you the conviction to pursue your visions.

- **Master your emotions.** Fear and self-doubt feel like facts but in actuality they are emotions that are only as powerful as they are allowed to be. Recognize these thoughts as emotions and do not allow them to twist your reality. Recognizing fear can help you master it.
- **Stop comparing yourself.** Embark on what makes you different and become the best you. Everyone has their talents; all it takes is to find yours and do what you are meant to do.

Fear of not being good enough is a mind-set—it is not reality. The way an entrepreneur can change and overcome this common fear is through self-reflection, positive self-talk and supportive relationships.

5. **Fear of success** is more common than we think. Entrepreneurs are faced with new challenges they have never encountered before. As the risks get higher so does the fear of success and all the other fears combined.

As Perell says, "We are worried about what will be different in our lives if we actually succeed. Trust that you'll be able to rise to the occasion, just like you have in the past when you were working to get your business off the ground. Build a team of strong people you can lean on and learn from. Focus on what success can offer, such as financial and creative freedom. And allow yourself to celebrate the successes you experience! Enjoy how awesome it is to have your hard work and passion be rewarded."

"I have felt all five of these fears throughout my career—and to be honest, I still feel them from time to time. But I don't let them dictate my life and stop me from moving forward, I'm way more scared of standing still."

Source: https://www.entrepreneur.com/article/353219, July 16, 2020

What Happens When Entrepreneurs Deal with Conflict?

Before we understand what happens when entrepreneurs deal with conflict, it is important to understand what conflict is about. Traditionally, research has identified conflict in terms of opposite interests between two individuals or parties. Opposing interest in conflict evolved out of limited resources, goal incongruence, anger, personal grudge, individual gain, favoritism and lack of people skills. Conflict also leads the individuals or parties to foster bigger conflicts (Mack and Synder, 1957; Pondy, 1967; Schmidt and Kochan, 1972).

Jehn and Bendersky (2003) defined conflict as perceived incompatibilities between two or more partners. Another view of perceived incompatibilities was raised in other research. De Dreu et al. (1999) argued that the creation of tension as a personal experience on account of perceived differences among the parties also needs to be considered as part of defining the term conflict.

In the end, an entrepreneurial venture is an organization either big or small with employees who have varied backgrounds, qualifications, experiences, specializations and team up with one another to accomplish the goals and vision created by the founder, a first-generation entrepreneur.

The spirit of the entrepreneur drives the entrepreneur to scale up and expand the entrepreneurial venture. Expansion, diversification, merger, acquisition and Initial Public Offers are always possibilities for significant growth enhancement. The attainment of founder's vision in the long run also becomes a reality, gradually.

Cooperative behavior is the best way to work to achieve mutually agreed-on goals. A study conducted by Chen and Tjosvold (2005) supports this idea. Chinese employees in different Chinese companies in various industries were working with their foreign managers at different levels and functional areas. The results indicate the increased leader-member exchange relationship and effectiveness of leadership, commitment, agreeableness and broad-minded discussions to deal with incoherent cultural views facilitated cooperative goals among Chinese employees and their foreign managers. Work cohesiveness among managers and employees improves significantly when employee engagement and involvement become the norm in the entrepreneurial venture. This leads to the formation of a culture of cooperative behavior in the long run. Similar studies conducted in Asia and North America revealed the significant role of cooperative and competitive conflict (Tjosvold, 2006).

Idea generation, creativity, cooperation, coordination, motivation, encouragement, support and care for others are some of the common characteristics of a well ran entrepreneurial venture. Both managers and employees have their own intellectual capabilities and personalities which differentiates us from one another. Even when we work together as part of a formal organization, we tend to voice our opinions, arguments, demands and requests to seek ethical conduct and individual justice.

Well-functioning organization depends on the kind of employees hired, vision of the cofounder(s), entrepreneurial leadership of entrepreneur, external investors, suppliers, distributors, creditors, retailers, resource availability, legal compliance and the venture's financial strength. An entrepreneur wants to have committed employees and other stakeholders. Occasionally, the decision of the entrepreneur may not be acceptable to the employees, either individually or in groups. Employees would like to have a culture of employee participation in management decisions whenever possible. While this is a good way to work collaboratively, it is practically impossible to implement. Unfortunate and bitter relationships between employer and employee can lead to major conflicts; the results of which could take the form of poor company morale and financial loss.

Disagreements may also occur between the entrepreneurial founders(s) and the cofounder(s) of the same entrepreneurial venture. Since the cofounders care for the entrepreneurial venture, they want the best for the organization. It is common for the cofounders to perceive the contexts and situations differently which in turn can lead to the individual dissatisfaction and disappointment that also causes conflicts affecting the stakeholders, directly or indirectly.

Disagreements also occur between the entrepreneurial founder(s) and other external stakeholders such as suppliers, distributors, wholesalers, retailer and government bodies. It is up to the entrepreneur to find solutions to this conflict situation. The most important aspect of the solution is the approach taken by the entrepreneur to avoid any type of conflict. The approach to the conflict is a point for the entrepreneur to become successful in the entrepreneurial process.

Nature and Sources of Conflict

To organize, operate and promote the vision of the entrepreneurial venture, the entrepreneur must have good interpersonal skills to manage the resources, people and technology in dealing with both the internal and external stakeholders. Conflict is unavoidable. But conflict can turn out to be potentially productive for the entrepreneur and the other stakeholders involved in the disagreement. Primarily, conflict occurs when the entrepreneurs, employees, venture capitalists, incubation managers, government regulatory representatives, angel investors, suppliers, distributors and retailers make a different choice from the available alternative courses of action. Conflict is a perceptual dynamic process and indicates a series of erratic and subtle events. It is a perceptual phenomenon. The perceptual differences between the parties in disagreement lead to conflict.

An entrepreneur confronts different but complex situations in the life of his/her entrepreneurial venture(s). Issues related to funds arrangement, employees' salaries and benefits, legal compliance, maintaining quarterly growth targets, building cohesive teams, keeping employees motivated, work-life balance, dealing with customers' concerns and satisfaction, and expenditures on data analytics and technologies consume a considerable amount of time, effort and energy. Since the entrepreneur has to manage and look after the various managerial and operational activities of the entrepreneurial venture, it is natural for the entrepreneur to confront various conflicts.

Research on organizational conflict over the last three decades provided an understanding of the functional and dysfunctional effects of conflict. The findings show the effects of conflict pertaining to group dynamics and performance outcomes of the organization (Amason, 1996; De Dreu and van Vianen, 2001; De Dreu and Weingart, 2003; Jehn, 1995, 1997; Lovelace et al., 2001). Also, positive effects of task conflict on the productivity measures were found (Amason, 1996; De Dreu and van de Vliert, 1997; Jehn, 1997). However, the effects of relationship conflict had a negative impact on the individual's well-being and team performance (Chen and Chang, 2005; De Dreu and van Vianen, 2001; Simons and Peterson, 2000).

It is interesting to note the other possible conflicts in an entrepreneurial venture. Conflict often occurs between the entrepreneur and the venture capitalist (VC). The relations are often different due to the conflicting interests and disagreements on various issues about the entrepreneur and the entrepreneurial venture. Both have their own conception of the firm and interpret the contractual terms from their own perspective. The level of involvement shown by VC in the entrepreneurial venture and the perception of VC about the performance of the entrepreneur, employees, products/services, customers' response, market demand and competitors' performance are the main areas of conflict between the VC and the entrepreneur (Yitshaki, 2008). This conflict is extremely intense when money is involved such as when a third party offers to buy the venture.

Types of Conflict

As mentioned earlier, conflict is unavoidable. It can be good or bad based on the functional or dysfunctional nature or the conflict experienced by the entrepreneur and other parts of the entrepreneurial ecosystem. The entrepreneur needs to tackle the conflicting interests tactfully to contain and minimize the conflict. The focus and energy of all the stakeholders of the entrepreneurial venture must be guided in the same direction. Conflict in the entrepreneur's lifecycle constantly increases as the venture seeks to improve and achieves priorities that affect the welfare of all stakeholders: quality products/services, financial performance, employee satisfaction, employee productivity, organizational growth, cost-effective measures and employee welfare and benefits to generate maximum return to fund providers and increase the value of investments.

The entrepreneur deals with the conflicting issues on a daily basis. These issues could range from meeting deadlines, as well as the expectations of the partners and VCs, procuring and managing raw materials from suppliers, planning and agreeing on distribution strategies, convincing partners and senior colleges pricing, marketing and promotional expenditures, as well as the need to invest in prototyping new innovative products. Besides these potential conflicts and threats, one should not be surprised to see the entrepreneur or an employee lashing out at a colleague who constantly undermines him/her and disregards his/her contributions leading to potential conflicts.

There are three types of conflicts across the entrepreneurial ecosystem that the entrepreneurs deal with: (a) task conflict, (b) relationship conflict and (c) value conflict. Conflict related to the task, work, process, system, procedure, rules, guidelines, instructions, policy measures and disciplinary steps of the organization fall in the category of the task conflict. All the stakeholders of the entrepreneurial venture, including the entrepreneur, know that task conflict is more important to the well-being of the organization. Task conflicts do need to be encouraged to a certain degree to reap the benefits of generating novel ideas, innovative products and services, cutting-edge technological solutions, innovative business models, promising new revenue streams, efficient supply chain management and logistics, diversifying in different emerging industries and developing new potential markets.

More often than not, task conflict helps the entrepreneur. The entrepreneur often becomes the de facto mediator between the individual and parties in conflicts. It helps the entrepreneur to understand the deeper interests in the ongoing conflicts. Such conflicting issues offer the entrepreneur a wider and balanced perspective.

In the beginning, the entrepreneur or other stakeholders acknowledges the conflict as a task conflict. The challenge is not to rule out the possibility of a task conflict turning into a relationship conflict. Since the relationship conflict takes over between the parties involved, the task conflict gets cast aside. The relationship conflict occurs primarily due to the individual differences, such as personality, conflict styles, perception, individual priorities and personal biases. The relationship conflict reflects the culture of an enterprise. The individual differences stimulate new thinking, creativity and a familiarity with the issues and concerns which may affect some of the members of the organization.

Relationship conflict allows the members to experience unconventional and a clearer view of others. It affects the interpersonal relationships of the involved parties in the conflict. Relationship conflicts focus on individual differences. These individual differences increase internal rivalry, jealousy, envy, superiority/inferiority complex as well as other behavioral issues. These behavioral issues hinder the functioning of the entrepreneurial venture by deviating employees from the goals and vision of the enterprise.

The third type of conflict, value conflict, occurs when the individual values, ethics and moral principles are compromised. For instance, if the entrepreneur or the senior members of the entrepreneurial venture becomes involved in fraudulent activities or suspicious dealings and transactions, the employees or other stakeholder of the enterprise with higher moral values may point out the wrongdoing. Several studies showed unethical practices in various enterprises. The employees felt violated by the immoral conduct of the management. The employees voiced their deeper ethical concerns or became whistle-blowers to highlight the malpractices (Babu, 2017). Prof. Lawrence Susskind mentioned that value-driven conflicts are likely to heighten defensiveness among parties and widened the gap between these three types of conflicts; the value conflict is the hardest to resolve because the involved parties are likely to stand by their core values.

Approaches to Conflict Management

Methods

Management of conflict is a major concern for every enterprise. In an entrepreneurial venture, the entrepreneur is expected to manage the conflict through effective methods and strategies. Studies confirmed that methods such as training, workshops, self-other awareness, participative management, communication and avoiding emotional issues have been effective in dealing with conflict issues among members of the organization. Models of conflict have also been developed to reduce the intensity of conflict and normalize the situation. Videoplayback (Alger, 1976), cross-confrontation (Paul, 1976) and conflict-resolution family therapy (Minuchin, 1965) were some of the early models of managing conflict. Walton (1969) proposed a model of conflict with the major elements: (1) positive attitude and motivation toward one another, (2) stability in situation power maintained by the two parties, (3) alignment of efforts of the partners, (4) restoring the dialogical smoothness by mitigating the differences and integrating the commonalities, (5) establishment of reliable and trustworthy communication channels and (6) efforts for open dialogue.

Models

The behavior-modification approach to conflict management is another model (Miller and Zoradi, 1977). It is comprised of recognition and definition of the problem, commitment, identifying the pleasant and unpleasant behaviors, negotiation, contract and follow-up. Different models of conflict emerged; Roark and Wilkinson (1979) mentioned a conflict management model in their book title "Group & Organization Studies." The model was propounded by Osgood (1962, 1969) for managing conflict. It is known as GRIT (Graduated Reciprocation in Tension-Reduction). The GRIT model applies communication channels, learning theories and principles to manage the conflict. Gordon's model became one of the most widely accepted models of conflict. The model allowed both sides to win by making the situation acceptable to both parties.

Styles

Thomas and Kilmann (1974) proposed a conflict model instrument. It had five styles or approaches to conflict management and included a self-assessment tool to assess an individual's own style of conflict. Even after several decades, the self-assessment tool is still relevant in today's business and entrepreneurial environment. The model is based on the fact that every individual falls into one of five conflicting styles when involved in a conflict. The challenge is to deal with the situations that are complex and dynamic in nature. What might work really well for an individual as the preferred conflicting style may not work equally as well in a different situation and/or with a different set of people. The research uses the five different styles of conflict management to understand the different situations in the light of the most appropriate style. It helped to understand the pros and cons of each situation of conflict and understand to apply these five styles of conflict to manage the conflicting situation professionally.

Table 2.1 Model of conflict.

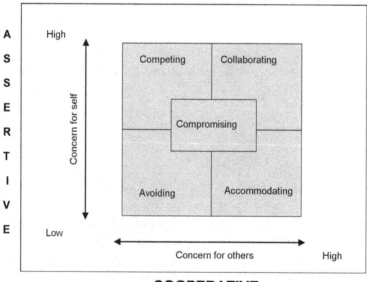

Source, modified from: https://sourcesofinsight.com/conflict-management-styles-at-a-glance/

As indicated in Table 2.1, the five styles of conflict management are: collaborating, competing, compromising, accommodating and avoiding. The collaboration style is the most ideal style of conflict as it strives for a win-win solution for both parties involved in the conflict. It should be chosen if there is no urgency in arriving at a decision, more people are involved or past attempts to resolve the conflict have failed. Collaboration style is not recommended if there is urgency in the decision-making process. It is also not recommended if the conflicting issue is perceived as too menial and less important for the majority of the individuals involved in the conflict.

Competition style of conflict expects the individual to take the firmest possible stand by safeguarding one's own priorities and goals at the cost of the other parties' loss. This can generate assertion in an individual which often sparks aggression in the opposition. When aggression is perceived, this individual also gets blamed for the failure to resolve the conflict. The competing style can be appropriate when the decision needs to be arrived at quickly. The competing style may also be appropriate if the other individual tries to take undue advantage of the situation. While one needs to be firm in taking the stand and upfront in making the demands, when members are found to be sensitive about the matter, competition style should be avoided.

Compromising style of conflict is significantly different. Each individual partially agrees to give up their own priorities and demands in the compromising style of conflict management. The reason to agree with the demands of the other party could be to attain larger objectives such as resolving the conflict at any cost. Unwillingness to escalate the conflict further could also be a larger objective. The compromising style is recommended if the decision is to be made soon. If the conflict resolution is the top priority rather than worrying about each member's individual priorities, then the compromising style is usually very appropriate. However, the style is not recommended if the stakes are too high and a variety of important needs must be addressed. The compromising style is also not recommended if there is power imbalance between the individuals and the situation demands an urgent solution.

The accommodating style is a passive style of conflict management due to an individual's approach to give-in to the demands of the other party. This could be due to the emotional factor or the influence of one party or member(s) over the other party or its member(s). The accommodating style does not do much to safeguard one's own priorities and demands. In certain situations, accommodating style is appropriate in maintaining good rapport with the other party, if the issue of the conflict is highly important for only one party. The accommodating style is not recommended in complex and dynamic issues of conflicts.

The avoiding style of conflict management is the last style. The term signifies that individuals prefer to avoid the conflict situation. The individual does not want to face the difficult situation due to a lack of confidence and courage or has an ulterior motive. This avoiding individual tends to delegate tasks to others and avoids making decisions. The avoiding is a style that would not be effective in managing conflict. Occasionally, the style is useful, provided the matter is trivial or the individual wants to delay the decision intentionally. If the outcome of the conflict is needed immediately, the team should never adopt the avoiding style of conflict.

The parties involved in any conflict must be well acquainted with the methods, models and the style of conflict management. In the entrepreneurial ecosystem, the entrepreneur must be capable enough to handle all the other stakeholder, including senior management, employees, VCs, suppliers, distributors, creditors, wholesalers, retailers, customers, government representatives and competing enterprises in the most respectful manner. The entrepreneur must establish trust, transparency and empathy for others while running the enterprise. A small discord with any one of these stakeholders mentioned above, if ignored, could seriously threaten the smooth functioning of the enterprise and affect its growth trajectory in the long run.

Chapter Summary

Entrepreneurship is an attractive proposition for all those aspiring to solve the problems of customers. With innovative ideas and available resources, people with a variety of skill sets can start the entrepreneurial journey. The most important achievement of launching and growing an enterprise for an entrepreneur is the autonomy and ownership of the enterprise. While nurturing the entrepreneurial venture, the entrepreneur touches base with several categories of experts and specialists. These people become associated with the enterprise at different levels and capacities. They offer various solutions, starting from the raw materials to the supply of components, machinery to financial assistance in the form of angel investment and venture financing to market research to strategic expertise often provided by serial entrepreneurs in order to scale up the entrepreneurial venture.

It is necessary for the entrepreneur to make strategic decisions and engage in various activities, such as extensive rounds of discussion, financial analyses, assessments, future projections, quarterly and annual reviews and alternative business plans. Entrepreneurial leadership, clear vision, effective business model, revenue streams and positive customer appeal attract the needed stakeholders to be involved in the start and growth of the entrepreneurial venture. Each has a keen interest in collaborating with the entrepreneur for the launch and growth of the entrepreneurial venture in the long run.

The entrepreneurial path has always been challenging with a lot of uncertainty. While the entrepreneur engages in various entrepreneurial activities, it is not uncommon that there are numerous entrepreneurial barriers. Barriers such as psychological, sociological, cultural and technological affect the entrepreneurial process of venture creation and development. It is essential for the entrepreneur to develop the skills to deal with individual and socially driven recurring and complex barriers. Entrepreneurship training, workshops, mentoring and incubation all assist in building a strong entrepreneurial orientation.

Eventually, all the barriers to entrepreneurship lead to some level of conflict. As an entrepreneur, one needs to learn ways to tackle different conflicting situations without burning any bridges. Some of the major types of conflict have been categorized as task conflict, relationship conflict and value conflict. Task conflict emphasizes the structure and processes of the conflict. It focuses on the problem of origin to solve the conflict. Relationship conflict is different. The entrepreneur in a relationship conflict knowingly or unknowingly engages in emotions and sentiments and thus can rupture the bonding and relationship. It is sometimes very difficult to emerge from such a complex situation primarily driven by relationship conflict. Value conflict is centered on values, ethics and moral principles of an entrepreneur and other members of the entrepreneurial venture. While solving the issues, conflicting situations and multiple vested interests arise. Such conflicting situations center on the value system and ethical functioning of the enterprise as a whole. Therefore, it becomes all the more challenging to derive a creative solution from value conflicts.

Approaches to a conflict help the entrepreneur understand the different methods, models and style of conflicts in the entrepreneurial ecosystem. Either through formal training or industry experience, an entrepreneur must cultivate the skills required to manage and resolve conflicts between the entrepreneur and various other groups such as the entrepreneur vs VC, entrepreneur vs suppliers, distributors, wholesalers, retailers, digital platform owners, employee vs employee or one department vs another department just to name a few. Conflict management skills are one of the most in-demand skills for the entrepreneur. The skills are important in dealing with all types of situations involving conflicting interests. It could be starting from convincing the family to start the venture, the inception of the entrepreneurial venture; seeking participation and contributions from experts, specialists and entrepreneurship mentors; seeking financial resources from different sources, managing physical resources, infrastructure and technological issues; dealing with employees' complaints and grievances; and dealing with issues involved in seeking cooperation with external stakeholders.

Key Terms

- Approaches to conflict management
- Barriers to entrepreneurship
- Conflict and its nature
- Sources of conflict
- Types of conflict

Review Questions

Q.1 Discuss the major barriers to entrepreneurship. What should be done by the entrepreneur to overcome such barriers?

Q.2 Identify some of the major challenges faced by the entrepreneur when confronting conflict.

Q.3 Broadly explain the nature and sources of conflict. Cite an example of the conflict which occurred between you and the other members. The members could be your family, relative or any other professional. Elaborate on ways you handled the conflict.

Q.4 Highlight the types of conflict. Based on your past experience in dealing with conflicts, analyze in detail the type of conflict in which you were involved.

Q.5 Discuss the methods, models and styles of conflict management. How useful is it to fully understand the conflict mechanism to deal with any type of conflict?

Q.6 Prepare a list of top 10 corporate conflicts by surfing the internet. Review the list of conflicts and categorize them based on the type of conflicts.

You Be the Entrepreneur

Before the retirement of Ratan Tata, ex-Chairman of Tata Sons and Tata Group, Cyrus Mistry was nominated as Chairman, Tata Group, from 2012 to 2016. However, in October 2016, the board of Tata Group's holding company, Tata Sons, voted to remove Cyrus Mistry as the Chairman. Post-removal of Mistry, former Chairman Rata Tata joined back as the interim Chairman of Tata Group and remained the Chair until 2017 when N. Chandrasekaran was made the Chairman. Cyrus Mistry felt strongly that the board's decision to remove him from the position of Chairman, Tata Sons, was not justified. The case was filed by Mistry challenging the decision at National Company

Law Appellate Tribunal (NCLAT). The court did not accept the appointment of N. Chandrasekaran as Executive Chairman and termed it illegal and restored Cyrus Mistry. The supreme court stayed the order of NCLAT in January 2020. In response, Mistry filed a cross appeal to the supreme court.

Background

The background uncovers several reasons for such a corporate-level conflict between one of the most celebrated industrialist Ratan Tata, who is a well-educated, experienced, knowledgeable businessman, and Cyrus Mistry. Some of the major reasons have been identified for this conflict that shook up the entire Indian corporate world.

The conflict of interest emerged in the initial months of the joining of Cyrus Mistry. He proposed to raise funds for the state election of Orissa. Since the early days, the Tata Group was receiving its iron ores from the state of Orissa. Thus, it was considered to be against the interest of the board to fund parliamentary elections. Mistry appointed directors of the board from external sources and offered them high salaries, commissions and perks. This caught the attention of the board as the new directors appointed by Mistry were paid millions of dollars in fees and commissions, even when the companies represented by these newly appointed directors were having huge financial losses.

While serving as the Chairman, Mistry was found to be instrumental in awarding the contracts of Tata Power and TCS worth US $300 million to his own family-run business, SO Corporation. When he joined the company and board, he had agreed to separate himself from the family-run business. Such a breach of trust was considered by the board as defaulting on the promise made by Mistry at the time of taking the position of chairman, which reflected the bad governance by Mistry.

Another major conflicting issue was the decision to acquire the company assets of Welspun Energy for US $544 million. The decision was not discussed with the board. Mistry did not seek any approval from them or investors as well. The decision came as a shock to the entire board when they were formally informed later.

Further, it is interesting to understand the criticism leveled at the board by Mistry. He criticized the board for not adhering to the clauses in Articles of Association which resulted in problems with the minority shareholders. He also criticized the Tata Trust for its involvement in trivial issues that led to numerous disagreements and conflicts. He felt that the Tata Group was mismanaged. The decisions are generally taken by Tata Sons Limited, resulting in negligible participation by the minority shareholders.

Currently, the conflict between the two parties is still in the court of law.

Source: "Tata-Ministry feud: Three incidents that lead to Cyrus' ouster from Tata Sons" by Shantanu Guha Ray, December 2016, www.firstpost .com

Case Scenario

Mycab is a ridesharing entrepreneurial venture started by entrepreneur Sylvester Goldsmith in 2015. The entrepreneurial venture established its office in the Silicon Valley, California, USA. Sylvester is 24 years old. Since his childhood, he has been extremely creative and studious. His personality was introvert by nature. He had limited friends from the early days of his school.

Sylvester earned his MBA in Entrepreneurship and Innovation from Babson College in USA in 2012. Before joining his MBA program, Sylvester had several creative ideas which he wanted to explore further to solve human problems and meet the customers' needs. As part of several entrepreneurship projects, accelerator programs and elevator pitches, Sylvester presented entrepreneurial ideas and business plans to mentors and angel investors for genuine feedback and valuable input. Post-MBA, having worked with a startup venture for three years, Sylvester decided to start his own enterprise. Mycab was born in May 2015. Sylvester was the founder and CEO. He already discussed his carsharing idea of Mycab with his few classmates in the MBA program who were also keen to join his enterprise. They wanted to add value through their expertise and experience working in corporations. Sylvester understood that the newborn enterprise needed experienced and seasoned entrepreneurs to offer mentoring support to Sylvester and his team. He sensed their vital role and contributions in strategizing the growth of the enterprise in the near future. Sylvester and his teammates decided to bring on board four senior executives who had 15–20 years of experience in nurturing and financing entrepreneurial ventures in a variety of industries. He and his team initially hired 17 employees. Later, they added another 12 employees to the payroll. The hired employees were in positions at middle and junior-level management in the hierarchical structure of the organization. Their roles did reflect the proper implementation and operationalization of functional divisions of the enterprise.

As a result, the enterprise started well. Sylvester's vision as an entrepreneur and founder, the cross-functional capabilities of his core team, leadership capabilities of the senior executives and support from all the employees helped the enterprise grow exponentially over the next three years. The growth rate has not decreased significantly in the last five years.

Six months ago, the top-level management started experiencing a unique challenge. Senior executives were found to be unhappy and frustrated with one another. They were also frustrated with the founder and CEO, Sylvester. Moreover, the employees who were working in the enterprise from the beginning wanted to quit their jobs. In one of the recent board meeting, senior executives exchanged heated arguments with Sylvester and his teammates on strategic planning and product marketing initiatives. The senior executives were not in agreement with Sylvester and his supporters regarding the decision made by Sylvester, being the CEO of the enterprise. By evening, two of the executives tendered their resignation. The HR manager informed Sylvester that he learned through the grapevine that seven of the employees were planning to tender resignation by early next week. Sylvester could not figure out the reasons. He failed to understand the right approach to tackle such an unprecedented scenario. He is now at a juncture not knowing how to confront his senior executives and his seven experienced employees. They may leave the organization if he does not respond with solutions soon.

The enterprise has been running successfully over the last five years. If you were to assume the position of Sylvester, the founder and CEO, Mycab, how would you respond and resolve the conflicts between the two categories of parties—senior executives vs the CEO and the employees vs the CEO?

Suggested Readings

1. Conflict management in entrepreneurship

Conflict Management in Entrepreneurship. (2020). Emerald Publishing Limited.

This book answers the conflict management issues in entrepreneurship management in the current digital economy. This book addresses the important but underexplored issues with different perspectives on the research area—Conflict Management in Entrepreneurship. It provides new research findings on conflict and entrepreneurship or new ventures for both emerging economies and mature economies.

2. Entrepreneurial attitude and conflict management through business simulations

Arias-Aranda, D., & Bustinza-Sánchez, O. (2009). Entrepreneurial attitude and conflict management through business simulations. *Industrial Management & Data Systems*, 109(8), 1101–1117.

This paper elucidates the influence that participation in a simulation experience based on the automobile industry has on the entrepreneurial attitude (entrepreneurship attitude orientation) through conflict management learning. This paper contributes to increasing knowledge in conflict management for workgroups maintaining intensive and relentless relationships over a relatively long period of time in which the simulation develops.

3. Venture capitalist-entrepreneur conflicts: An exploratory study of determinants and possible resolutions

Yitshaki, R. (2008), "Venture capitalist-entrepreneur conflicts: An exploratory study of determinants and possible resolutions," *International Journal of Conflict Management*, Vol. 19 No. 3, pp. 262–292.

This article examines the inherent and actual conflicts between VCs and entrepreneurs, as well as the possible resolutions of these conflicts. The findings provide an insight into the dynamic nature of conflicts between VCs and entrepreneurs.

4. A model of destructive entrepreneurship: insight for conflict and post-conflict recovery

Desai, S., Acs, Z. J., & Weitzel, U. (2013). A Model of Destructive Entrepreneurship: Insight for Conflict and Postconflict Recovery. Journal of Conflict Resolution, 57(1), 20–40.

This article proposes three assumptions to develop a model of destructive entrepreneurship that presents the mechanisms through which entrepreneurial talent behaves in an unproductive manner. The article also presents four key propositions on the nature and behavior of destructive entrepreneurship. Research agendas and policy streams, with a focus on relevance to conflict and post-conflict recovery, are discussed in the end.

5. Conflict between the VC and entrepreneur: The entrepreneur's perspective

Andrew Zacharakis, Truls Erikson & Bradley George (2010) Conflict between the VC and entrepreneur: the entrepreneur's perspective, Venture Capital, 12:2, 109-126, DOI: 10.1080/13691061003771663

In this study, the effects of conflict on confidence in partner cooperation are explored. While the literature on VC–entrepreneur interactions is well developed, viewing the impact of conflict within the dyad is less developed. The implications of the findings suggest that it is important for the entrepreneurial team to build cohesion both within the team and with the VC so that if a conflict arises, it does not lead to lower overall performance.

References

Alger, I. (1976). 'Integrating immediate video playback in family therapy'. In P. J. Guerin, Jr., (Ed.), *Family therapy: Theory and practice*. New York: Gardner Press, pp. 530–533.

Ameson, A. C. (1996). 'Distinguishing the effects of functional and dysfunctional conflict on strategic decision-making: Resolving a paradox for top management'. *Academy of Management Journal*, Vol. 39, No. 1, pp. 123–148.

Babu, V. (2017). 'Examining the dilemma between ethical misconduct of individuals and the talent selection process at CBCBC Global Bank'. *Journal of Service Research*, Vol. 17, No. 2, pp. 41–53.

Birch, D. L. (1979). *The Job Generation Process MIT Programme on Neighbourhood and Regional Change*. Cambridge, MA: MIT Press.

Boettke, P. J. and Coyne, C. J. (2008). 'The political economy of the philanthropic enterprise'. In G. E. Shockley, P. M. Frank, & R. R. Stough (Eds.), *Non-market entrepreneurship*. Edward Elgar Publishing, Cheltenham, UK; Northampton, MA.

Chen, M., and Chang, Y. (2005). 'The dynamics of conflict and creativity during a project's life cycle: A comparative study between service-driven and technology-driven teams in Taiwan'. *International Journal of Organizational Analysis*, Vol. 13, No. 2, pp. 127–150.

Chen, M., and Tjosvold, D. (2005). 'Cross cultural leadership: Goal interdependence and leader-member relations in foreign ventures in China'. *Journal of International Management*, Vol. 11, pp. 417–439.

De Dreu, C. K. W., Harinck, F., and Van Vianen, A. E. M. (1999). 'Conflict and performance in groups and organizations'. In Cooper, C. L., and Robertson, I. (Eds.), *International Review of Industrial and Organizational Psychology*, No. 14. Indianapolis, IN: Wiley, pp. 369–414.

De Dreu, C. K. W., and van de Vliert, E. (1997). *Using Conflict in Organizations*. London: Sage Publications.

De Dreu, C. K. W., and Van Vianen, A. E. M. (2001). 'Managing relationship conflict and the effectiveness of organizational teams'. *Journal of Organizational Behaviour*, Vol. 22, No. 3, pp. 309–328.

De Dreu, C. K. W., and Weingart, L. R. (2003). 'Task versus relationship conflict, team performance, and team member satisfaction: A meta-analysis'. *Journal of Applied Psychology*, Vol. 88, pp. 741–749.

Desai, M., Gompers, P., and Lerner, J. (2003). *Institutions, Capital Constraints and Entrepreneurial Firm Dynamics: Evidence From Europe*. NBER Working Paper No. 10165. Cambridge, MA: NBER.

Gordon, T. (1970). *Parent Effectiveness Training*. New York, NY: Wyden.

Jehn, K. A. (1995). 'A multi-method examination of the benefits and detriments of intra group conflict'. *Administrative Science Quarterly*, Vol. 40, No. 2, pp. 256–282.

Jehn, K. A. (1997). 'Affective and cognitive in work groups: Increasing performance through value-based intragroup conflict'. In De Dreu, C. K. W., and van de Vliert, E. (Eds.), *Using Conflict in Organizations*. London: Sage Publication, pp. 87–100.

Jehn, K. A., and Bendersky, C. (2003). 'Intragroup conflict in organizations: A contingency perspective on the conflict-outcome relationships'. *Research in Organizational Behaviour*, Vol. 25, pp. 187–242.

Klapper, L., Laeven, L., and Rajan, R. (2006). 'Entry regulations as a barrier to entrepreneurship'. *Journal of Finance Economics*, Vol. 82, No. 3, pp. 591–629.

Lorrain, J and Laferté, S. (2006). 'Support needs of the young entrepreneur'. *Journal of Small Business and Entrepreneurship*, Vol. 19, No. 1, pp. 37–48.

Lovelace, K., Shapiro, D. L., and Weingart, L. R. (2001). 'Maximizing cross-functional new product teams' innovativeness and constraint adherence: A conflict communication perspective'. *Academy of Management Journal*, Vol. 44, No. 4, pp. 779–793.

Mack, R. W., and Snyder, R. C. (1957). 'The analysis of social conflict – Toward an overview and synthesis'. *Journal of Conflict Resolution*, Vol. 1, pp. 212–248.

Miller, G. D., and Zoradi, S. D. (1977). 'Roommate conflict resolution'. *Journal of College Student Personnel*, Vol. 18, pp. 228–230.

Minuchin, S. (1965). 'Conflict-resolution family therapy'. *Psychiatry*, Vol. 28, No. 3, pp. 278–286.

Osgood, C. E. (1962). *An Alternative to War or Surrender*. Urbana, IL: University of Illinois Press.

Osgood, C. E. (1969). 'Calculated de-escalation as a strategy'. In Pruitt, D. C., and Snyder, R. C. (Eds.), *Theory and Research on the Causes of War*. Englewood Cliffs, NJ: Prentice Hall.

Paul, N. L. (1976). 'Cross-confrontation'. In P. J. Guerin, Jr., (Ed.), *Family therapy: Theory and practice*. New York: Gardner Press, pp. 520–521.

Pondy, L. R. (1967). 'Organizational conflict: Concepts and models'. *Administrative Science Quarterly*, Vol. 12, pp. 296–320.

Roark, A. E., and Wilkinson, L. (1979). 'Approaches to conflict management'. *Group & Organization Studies*, Vol. 4, No. 4, pp. 440–452.

Schmidt, S. M., and Kochan, T. A. (1972). 'Conflict: Toward conceptual clarity'. *Administrative Science Quarterly*, Vol. 85, No. 1, pp. 102–111.

Simon, T. L., and Peterson, R. S. (2000). 'Task conflict and relationship conflict in top management teams: The pivotal role of intragroup trust'. *Journal of Applied Psychology*, Vol. 85, No. 1, pp. 102–111.

Thomas, K. W., and Kilmnn, R. H. (1974). *The Thomas-Kilmann Conflict Mode Instrument*. Mountain View, CA: CPP, Inc.

Tjosvold, D. (2006). 'Defining conflict and making choices about management: Lighting the dark side of organizational life'. *International Journal of Conflict Management*, Vol. 17, No. 2, p. 91.

Yitshaki, R. (2008). 'Venture capitalist-entrepreneur conflicts: An exploratory study of determinants and possible resolutions'. *International Journal of Conflict Management*, Vol. 19, No. 3, pp. 262–292.

Chapter 3

COMMUNICATION SKILLS
FOR ENTREPRENEURS

Learning Objectives

1. To understand the importance of communication in conflict management
2. To describe how negotiation works toward forming the entrepreneurial skills
3. To highlight the key tactics of communication for effective negotiation
4. To discuss how non-verbal communication plays an important role while negotiating with the other party
5. To learn the key aspects of persuasion skills demonstrated by the negotiator in negotiation
6. To understand the role of influencing skills in negotiation and conflicts

OPENING SCENARIO: THE DISNEY-FOX MERGER

One of the greatest media acquisitions of all times started with two glasses of wine at the Mortgage Estate winery in California in late 2017. Host Rupert Murdoch, twenty-first century Fox chairman, and Disney President Bob Iger got along very well. As Iger said on CNBC: "We genuinely like each other and respect each other." A good start for a very discreet deal that only became known when it was almost done. The negotiations were conducted very quietly; even top executives of both companies were kept out of the loop. Once the market found out about it, Comcast (who owns NBCUniversal) made a counteroffer of $65 billion all cash.

Sony Pictures Entertainment and Verizon expressed interest, and Disney quickly topped up its original $52.4 billion offer to a staggering $71.3 billion showing the power of a strong alternative. Disney would only purchase the twenty-first century's entertainment asset, without its news and sports division. These divisions would be spun off into a New Fox.

But the acquisition was also problematic for Disney, as buying Fox would be a horizontal merger, meaning that the company buys another one offering the same products. Yet, regulators quickly confirmed the deal. The deal illustrates Disney's taste for consolidation. Disney already owned Lucasfilm, Marvel and Pixar.

Communication Skills and Conflict Management

Communication is vital for everyone; it occurs when an individual or a group share, inform, guide, tell, persuade, convey and influence the other individual or group of people to attain one or more objectives and goals. This exchange of thoughts, ideas, feelings and emotions is all part of the process of communication.

Communication is indeed an act of conveying meaning or transferring information from one location, individual or group to another. It involves primarily the sender, message, receiver and feedback. Communication is expected to bring clarity, transparency and trust between individuals or groups. Communication suffers when the process of communication is not well-established between the sender and receiver. This results in ambiguity and uncertainty among all the stakeholders, in turn, leading to poor communication and conflict.

Misunderstanding, disagreements and dissatisfactions often occur between the individuals or groups and eventually turn into conflicts. For instance, Steve Jobs, the founder of Apple, had an amazing ability to communicate with his audience. He always spoke with passion and communicated using a storytelling approach. His approach of communication made almost everyone to understand and connect positively with him, his dream and vision for Apple (Walker, 2011). While Steve Jobs is considered to be one of the greatest innovators in the history of innovation, he was also powerful in his communication skills. This helped him connect the dots and empathize with his customers around the world.

While poor communication ends up in conflicting situations, it also causes individuals to suffer due to the lack of clear and precise information about a situation. The intent of communication must be clear to the individual who sends the message to the receiver. The thoughts and ideas must be sensibly expressed in order for the other person to understand and respond well. Ironic and harsh words can be hurtful to others and, in turn, can spoil the relationship of individuals or groups. Avoiding such bitter situations ensures better communication with each other. However, this does not occur enough. People get annoyed and lose their temper. Poor communication can promote a culture of fear, threat, depression and major conflicts among individuals in society.

To manage the conflicts well, it is best that an individual experience it as well. As one experiences conflicts, the depth and level of conflicts become more apparent. Experience enables individuals to look at a particular conflict from different perspectives. One of the best ways to handle communication in conflict is to clearly express one's expectations to the other person. More often than not, we tend to have high expectations of others and are affected when these high expectations are overlooked or downplayed. Reacting too much to trivial matters affects the communication between individuals or groups.

Maintaining a normal pitch and tone helps make the communication better. To establish trust and transparency, communication is best done with each individual separately. To provide a bigger picture, a common platform needs to be developed to communicate the message or information to all. Using effective communication technologies such as emails and social media are sources of communication that are effective in maintaining transparency, accuracy and speed.

Working, collaborating and making good deals with other stakeholders bring thrill and excitement, especially at different levels of hierarchy in an entrepreneurial ecosystem. To perform well, strong communication skills are needed. Opponent parties always step forward with a rigid notion that there will occur a zero-sum game (Bazerman & Neale, 1983). In a real sense, integrative negotiations can allow the result to actually expand. This offers much more to every party involved in the conflict. Each party gets a higher outcome that benefits all the parties involved (Fisher & Ury, 1981). The entrepreneur must develop strong communication skills since conflict will occur in the entrepreneurial journey.

Jack and Symonds were two employees who worked in the design department of an entrepreneurial venture. While they were colleagues, often they disagreed with each other regarding ideas or suggestions about different areas of design. One week, the Head of the Design Department assigned a task to Jack to develop some new product designs by working with Symonds, his colleague. The innovative product designs were to be showcased through a proposed formal presentation a week later. When Jack discussed the newly assigned task with Symonds, there were many disagreements, in terms of choice of designs, process, product quality, cost and role in the presentation. When the head asked about the status of the presentation, Jack started complaining about Symonds for not cooperating. This infuriated the head and both were given a strong warning to work together. This experience made Jack and Symonds further annoyed and helpless as they did not want to work together. This eventually resulted in a large conflict that could have been at least partially avoided through effective communication.

Negotiation as an Entrepreneurial Skill

In the above example of Jack and Symonds, both of them did not want to work together which ended up in a large conflict. Lack of effective communication by both Jack and Symonds was evident. They lost the trust, empathy and transparency to work together. Rather, they had high egos and envy for each other. They did not want to see each other win. To restore trust, transparency, empathy and emotional stability, effective communication to balance the conflicting situation is called for. Negotiation, as an entrepreneurial skill, needs to be embedded in order to achieve success.

Negotiation is a universal skill. But all entrepreneurs do not have good negotiation skills to resolve the conflicts and develop good deals. However, entrepreneurs can learn negotiation skills by understanding and practicing negotiation strategies and tactics. Business professionals, diplomats, sportsmen, politicians, defense specialists and police personnel apply negotiation skills in their careers. They resolve difficult conflicts using negotiation skills.

Negotiation was defined as a process initiated by two or more opposition parties arriving at a common decision across several alternatives to a decision caused by the initial individual differences between them (Bazerman & Carroll, 1987; Kelley & Thibaut, 1978; Pruitt, 1981, 1983). In simple terms, negotiation is a constructive dialogue between two or more individuals or parties wanting to arrive at a common good agreement. By resolving the issues of conflict, negotiation turns out to be an effective way to balance the interests of both parties. It is a strategy to remove the deadlock or impasse in conflict and increase mutual gains through creative alternatives for both parties.

Communication plays a substantial role in the process of negotiation by conveying the intent and objectives to resolve the conflict. Different types and channels of communication are applied to cultivate a fertile ground for negotiation to take place. An entrepreneur can be a good negotiator by constantly practicing negotiation skills in complex situations of conflict. This can be achieved through patience and constant practice. An entrepreneur wanting to become a good negotiator needs to possess the important attributes, viz planning skills, clarity of thinking when pressured, verbal skills, understanding body language, organizational skills, technical knowledge of the products, persuasive skills, influencing skills, high integrity and trustworthiness, empathetic nature, perseverance and resilience to name a few.

As an entrepreneur, having state-of-the-art negotiation skills can help the entrepreneur understand the conflicts from a different perspective and guide the creation of the best deals with effective negotiations. Numerous entrepreneurs often do not succeed in their business life cycle due to their poor negotiation skills. Being a good negotiator, the entrepreneur has a better chance to resolve conflicts and develop good deals for the entrepreneurial venture.

The following are several examples in entrepreneurship that will help you learn the ways an entrepreneur negotiates with the stakeholders. One of the key stakeholders of an entrepreneurial venture is the supplier. Maintaining a cordial relationship with the suppliers is extremely important. Negotiation, in such cases, plays a strong role in securing good deals for the entrepreneur. The supplier relationships affect both the bottom line and top line of the entrepreneurial venture. Entrepreneur negotiates with the supplier on the terms of payment, the grant of exclusive territorial rights and the terms and conditions of the contract. The relationship between the entrepreneur and the supplier needs to be cultivated, keeping in mind the longer-term gains and benefits. More than just a line of communication, the state-of-the-art negotiation skills become powerful in extracting mutually agreeable outcomes. It sustains the positive, future relationships of stakeholders.

An increase in sales is key to the growth of any entrepreneurial venture. If the customers are not purchasing the products/services of the enterprise, the entrepreneur will be concerned. To keep financially strong in the entrepreneurial ecosystem, the entrepreneur needs to ensure an increase in annual sales. The sales team understands the role of negotiation skills in selling the products to business-to-business (B2B) or business-to-customer (B2C) markets. Negotiation skills impact retail sales. Non-monetary options such as commissions, discounts and concessions can be achieved by the sales team of the enterprise through effective negotiation skills.

Entrepreneurs need to be capable to guide and support the hiring of smart candidates for the entrepreneurial venture. If smart and committed employees are hired, the entrepreneur will witness the difference in terms of quality, quantity and speed of work. This will help the enterprise grow faster and bigger. The entrepreneur and the core team will need to negotiate with the candidates interested in joining the enterprise. The candidates' salaries, perks, incentives and employment contracts need to be negotiated to hire the best employees for the enterprise. Poor experience, failures and inconsistency of results in the past indicate that the company's performance will depend on the quality of hiring, training and evaluation of employees. Negotiation skills play an important role in increasing the quality of the dialogue between the entrepreneur and the hiring team, the candidates and the hiring team, the entrepreneur and the entire employee base.

Another critical area of negotiation of the entrepreneur is with funds providers such as venture capitalists (VC). Money is needed at many stages in the venture such as scale-up, expansion and diversification. If the agreements with the VCs are not well negotiated, problems can occur. Research has indicated that poor negotiation skills can cause the entrepreneur to lose control and ownership of the enterprise. Good negotiation skills can result in obtaining from the VC a better exit strategy for the VC, the involvement of VC in strategic decisions or influencing the other members of the venture and the rate of return on the investment.

Communication Secrets for Effective Negotiation

Several research studies have indicated the importance of the communication medium in negotiation. The communication medium is a significant factor in the processes and outcome of negotiation (Chen & Tseng, 2016; Galin et al., 2007; Geiger & Parlamis, 2014; Loewenstein et al., 2005; Purdy et al., 2000; Sheffield, 1995). An effective negotiator believes in the interaction of individuals involved to resolve a conflict. Interaction reveals the expectations of each to establish the terms of the agreement. (Lewicki et al., 2010). Regardless of the type of enterprise, the entrepreneur and his teams engage in negotiations regularly. It is necessary to understand that the negotiation and its successful outcome are primarily based on effective communication skills which lead to effective negotiations.

Hollingshead et al. (1993) research posits the presence of a high degree of complexity in a negotiation. It entails various subprocesses of communication including sending information, understanding the other party's arguments, presenting own arguments and checking the available offers from the other parties. These negotiations could be on strategic choices, employees' annual increments, attrition of employees, financial planning, fund-raising options, launching a new product line in the market, the types of marketing research, technology up-gradation, complying legal requirements and/or signing new or renewing contracts with suppliers, distributors and retailers.

Tactics play an important role in effective negotiation. These tactics work well when the entrepreneur is knowledgeable about effective communication. Non-verbal communication skills have become more important than verbal skills for a successful negotiation. Learning the subtle nuances of the non-verbal aspects of communication makes the entrepreneur mindful of how the other individual or party thinks and feels; the understanding of non-verbal communication allows the entrepreneur to learn how the other party sees the presence of the entrepreneur, their seriousness about the issues, priorities, ulterior motives, moods, feelings and emotions at the negotiating table. For instance, if the opponent is crossing arms across the chest means that the negotiator is not agreeing with what is being stated during the negotiation strategy. Such observations in non-verbal communication can help understand the mind-set and attitude of the opposition.

Unlike non-verbal cues, verbal communication is more apparent and can be observed. However, the entrepreneur who has never been a part of any negotiation process may not notice such verbal cues of the other parties. For instance, if the opponent negotiator raises his voice while negotiating, the purpose may likely be to make the first party feel afraid. The other parties would like to place some fear in the minds of the first party. It is an attempt to generate a sense of threat and to also indicate that the opponent negotiator is not afraid of the consequences if the negotiation fails.

Preparing for entrepreneurial negotiation is crucial in resolving the conflict and creating an agreement. It is the planning that matters most in negotiation. Planning an entrepreneurial negotiation should include ascertaining the demands, interests, concessions and offerings. Best Alternative to a Negotiated Agreement (BATNA), Zone of Possible Agreement (ZOPA), reservation value, Worst Alternative to a Negotiated Agreement (WATNA) are possible structural and psychological barriers to the negotiation.

Open-ended communications can be beneficial in negotiation. It encourages more open-ended questions with the other party. The purpose is to understand more about what and how the opposing party views the negotiation. The open-ended questions, such as "what" and "how," make the opponent elaborate on the issues or the pain points that need to be addressed. After having asked the open-ended questions, it is best to sit quietly and maintain silence for a few seconds. It will allow the opponent negotiator to ponder and respond, hopefully favorably. Open-ended communication can work best if it is planned thoroughly before the negotiation process begins. A negotiation skills checklist is found in Table 3.1.

Role of Non-Verbal Communication in Negotiation and Conflict Resolution

Negotiating with the other side is about defending and presenting one's demands and priorities without compromising the priorities of the opponent party. Non-verbal communication provides important cues on the opponent's negotiation tactics. Understanding the body language, which is a form of non-verbal communication of an individual, provides insight about the bodily gestures of an individual on the meanings of a situation, person or issue. An entrepreneur must learn to observe and read the body language of others.

Body language can help derive greater insights on an issue, based on the responses received from the opponent throughout the negotiations. An entrepreneur can observe some of the important aspects of the body language of

Table 3.1 Negotiation skills checklist.

	Questions	Yes
1	In negotiations, do people often take advantage of you?	
2	Do you struggle to have difficult conversations?	
3	Do you win negotiations but struggle to maintain business relationships?	
4	Do you let others win negotiations because you are uncomfortable with conflict?	
5	Do you avoid talking about price until the end?	
6	Do you avoid talking about difficult issues until the end?	
7	Do you know how to respond when, early in the negotiation, the other party says let's skip the haggling, just give me your best price?	
8	Do you know how to cope with there being another decision maker who is not present?	
9	Do you know how to deal with delaying tactics?	
10	Do you know the difference between positions and interests in a negotiation?	
11	Can you handle an aggressive negotiator?	
12	Do you know how to avoid "buyer s remorse" (when the buyer cancels the sale some time after you've agreed it)?	

Source: http://www.neilurquhart.com

the opponent while negotiating. First, an entrepreneur should observe the normal behavior of the opponent in the negotiation. Normal behavior is also called baseline behavior. It entails all the normal body language which is displayed when the individual is in a relaxed or neutral settings. Eye contact, pitch, tone of voice, smiles, hand movements and body postures are important aspects of body language. Body language that does not represent any stress, depression, anxiety, fear or pressure is considered the baseline behavior of an individual.

Failure to observe the normal or baseline behavior of the opponent negotiators could make an entrepreneur's observations regarding the body language incorrect. An entrepreneur would find it challenging to make decisions in the negotiation based on the misinterpretations in the body language. This could also cause one to fail to apply negation tactics as part of the negotiation planning. Due to the absence of knowledge of the normal baseline behavior of the opponent, an entrepreneur becomes less effective in negotiating the deal. It is highly recommended to have a talk with the other party before the formal process of negotiation begins. This helps the entrepreneur have adequate time to perceive by listening and observing the normal behavior represented in the opponent's body language.

Body language can also be known by the entrepreneur by observing minutely the engaging, disengaging and stress-driven body language of the opponent. Maintaining eye contact, paying attention, active listening, leaning forward and nodding of the opponent's head all indicate the body language which conveys the interests and willingness of the other party to resolve the conflict and negotiate the deal. The disengaged body language represents a casual approach. It entails a lack of interest, not paying attention, not listening properly, not replying fully, dodging the questions, ignoring the presence of others, switching to other topics, leaning back and narrowed eyes. Stress body language is completely different from engagement and disengagement body language. Stress body language entails anxiety, sarcasm, demeaning talks, uneasiness toward the progress of negotiation, nose-touching and a high pitched voice. Either the opponent negotiators are not interested in the outcomes of the negotiation or they have some other plans for the negotiation.

An entrepreneur should try to understand the body language by clustering them into different common groups. It helps the entrepreneur to derive the collective meaning of the clustered non-verbal communication. For example, the multiple body gestures, such as avoiding eye contact, pointing the feet toward the door and wet hands, collectively indicate that the opponent wants to quit the ongoing negotiation between the two parties and is desperate to leave the negotiation meeting.

It is not difficult for an entrepreneur to learn body language. He/she has been constantly exposed to non-verbal communication. We noticed several aspects of body language that remain in our unconscious mind. An entrepreneur needs to shift the body language from the unconscious mind to the awareness stage to apply this collective knowledge in real negotiations.

How Persuasion Helps in Negotiation?

Negotiation is all about the communication efforts put forth by the two individuals or parties at different stages of the conflict to achieve mutual understanding. While the two may share some interests, some interests remain opposite. To deal with those opposite interests between the individuals, persuasion skills play a vital role to convince the opponent or party. It works well when an effective negotiator sees the possibility of disagreement on some aspects being negotiated.

Persuasion skills are a psychological process different from negotiation skills. In negotiation, one tries to exchange resources for mutual gains and resolve conflict. Persuasion skills focus on changing the mind-set, attitude and beliefs of an individual about the interests and priorities in negotiation. The behavior of negotiation skills and persuasion skills are different. Negotiation is quick in approach despite several rounds of negotiation that may take place. Persuasion takes more time. It is slow in approach. Negotiation brings the two parties to the negotiating table, whereas persuasion is preferred at almost any level of the conflict.

In negotiation, the negotiator wants to establish a clear line of communication with the counterpart. By its very nature, persuasion cannot be direct. Rather, it contains subtle persuasive actions, movements and messages to convince and seek agreement from the opponent. The art of persuasion informs the effective negotiator to frame goals that build common ground between the opposing parties. In the negotiation process, the negotiator tries to persuade the other party based on this common ground (Conger, 1998). Rackham and Carlisle (1978a, b) substantiate the stated argument based on their research on effective negotiators. The good negotiators were found to be focusing on areas of disagreements and key issues of conflict. Contrarily, effective negotiators paid much more attention to the common ground.

Putting an offer on the negotiating table and waiting for the other party to respond is not sufficient for a win-win situation in the conflict. Persuading the opponent to change their views based on the merits and understanding the position of the opponent in the conflict require persuasion skills. It entails applying the tactics to change the mind-set, attitude, perception and beliefs of the opponent during the negotiation process. It can be developed through regular practice between colleagues and friends or by undergoing formal training in persuasion skills.

One of the techniques of persuasion is to ask the opponent to present their viewpoint followed by a question and answer session. Research has confirmed that the percentage of presenters who will present their views is likely to be low in number. Merely presenting our viewpoint will likely not change the viewpoint of others (Curran, 2020).

Another technique of persuasion is to ask questions during the negotiation. It is recommended to ask questions as the questioning approach enables the other party to feel free to open up, discuss and express what and how they feel about the matter being disputed. Essentially, the art of listening enables the negotiator to raise pertinent questions to the opponent. Listening helps turn the information into intelligence through close observation of words and tones used. The negotiating entrepreneur applies this knowledge to the advantage of both parties in the negotiation. Both persuasion and negotiation are complementary to each other even though their behaviors are different.

Presenting the viewpoints of the opponent and asking questions are two effective persuasive techniques in negotiation. Another important persuasive technique is to offer concessions. Concession means the negotiator is willing to give up a priority and agrees to let the opponent have what they have been demanding for a while, as part of the conflict resolution. Such concessions are agreed to by the parties to achieve more through long-term relationships and improve trust between them.

One of the tactics of persuading the opponent is delaying and not hurrying to concede to the other party. Responding by taking more time and intentionally delaying the opinions, viewpoints, actions and concessions provide the first negotiator ample opportunities to observe, understand, plan and decide how to persuade the opponent in the negotiation. Not hurrying could be a good persuasive tactic to win the negotiation. Negotiators must have a high level of patience. Patience helps the negotiator delay the offering of the first concessions to the opponent. The more time before the negotiator concedes to the other party, the more the opponent becomes impatient to have more. However, the negotiator should not always delay closing a deal. The negotiator should be mindful of the sensitive issues in the conflict as it affects the long-term relationship between the parties.

All these persuasive techniques help the entrepreneur become a good negotiator to complete deals and resolve conflicts throughout the entrepreneurial venture's creation, growth and development process.

Role of Influencing Skills in Negotiation

Influencing skills are needed in a successful negotiation. Influencing others is the ability to change others' way of thinking, attitude, mind-set or behavior as a whole or indirectly. Similar to influencing skills, persuasion requires an intentional but gradual approach to change the attitude or mind-set of others. However, influencing skills of an individual do not always intentionally make the other person feel the need to change their perspective. Rather, the individual inspires others indirectly through various acts.

Kipnis et al. (1980) posit influence tactics acting as an effective means to achieve one's goals in an organizational context. The authors' research indicates the desired goals of the negotiator to apply influence tactics to change the behavioral responses of the opponent.

Influence tactics are meant to change attitudes or actions concerning the target. Researchers classified behavioral change processes into three types: (1) personal identification, (2) compliance and (3) internalization. These processes drive the intended changes in attitude or action (Kelman, 1958; Yukl, 2013).

Influence tactics are effective instruments in negotiation. However, one of the influence tactics—pressure tactics—carries intentional pressure to elicit compliance from others. Since it generates a threat to the target, the target can opt to comply to avoid adverse consequences (Kelman, 1958; Yukl, 2013). Similarly, employees put pressure on their managers to support their goals. This cultivates an environment of mistrust and reactive behavior on the part of managers toward their subordinates (Blickle, 2003, 2004; Kipnis & Schmidt, 1988; Yukl et al., 1995; Yukl & Tracey, 1992). Research has confirmed that pressure-building attempts are ineffective influence tactics for individuals to attain their goals. Pressure-building tactics negatively affect the outcomes gleaned from trustworthy relationships, such as backing from senior-level executives (Lee et al., 2017).

Influencing others is challenging and more powerful than persuasion. It is an indirect and unintentional approach to inspire one's partners, negotiating opponents or other parties. The inspiration from the individual helps others to pursue something which they had not thought about doing. Influencing skills help in changing the mind-set or thought process of others toward a conflicting situation.

Cialdini (2007) discusses seven principles of influence. These principles— reciprocation, commitment, consistency, social proof, authority, liking and scarcity—are highly effective in influencing others in negotiation. An entrepreneur communicates with cofounders, VC, suppliers, distributors, retailers and customers as part of running the entrepreneurial venture. All such realms of communication need to include these seven principles of influence to get better and more meaningful outcomes in negotiation and conflict management.

An entrepreneur must have the influencing skills to impact the outcomes of a particular situation. If an entrepreneur possesses the influencing skills, it means that the entrepreneur is capable of getting "buy-in" from cofounders, colleagues, the senior management team, employees, VC, suppliers, distributors, creditors, wholesalers, retailers, customers and other entrepreneurs. Influencing skills consist of verbal and non-verbal communication and persuasion to inspire others. The personal brand of the entrepreneur helps in building credibility among opponents in negotiation. Inspiring others by one's good deeds, courage and confidence allows the entrepreneur to build one's brand over time. Influencing skills, therefore, are an indirect way of inspiring the opponent to become convinced of the deal or managing conflict.

Emotional Intelligence (EI) in business and entrepreneurship has become significant. Knowledge of EI makes the entrepreneur apply influencing skills in negotiation. To be ready with influencing skills, the entrepreneur needs to know the power dynamics between individuals or parties involved. Research has indicated that different influencing techniques adopted by a good negotiator while negotiating with the opponent can influence the outcome. Some of these techniques are logical reasoning, questioning, manipulating, using silent allies, forcing, ingratiation, legitimating, pressure, inspirational appeals, association, alliance building, appealing to values, modeling, socializing, empowerment and exchange. These are applied by a good negotiator to impact the outcomes of the negotiation. These influencing techniques can be broadly classified into four categories: rational category, emotional category, social category and dark side category. The nature of the situation, parties involved, power dynamics and negotiation skills of the negotiating opponents or parties are instrumental in determining the outcomes expected from an effective negotiation.

These aspects and their relationship to influencing are indicated in figure 3.1.

Chapter Summary

Effective communication skills help an entrepreneur express ideas, feelings, emotions, problem-solving and understanding others. It also allows openness, trust and transparency. The essence of successfully managing any conflict by an entrepreneur is based on communication channels, levels, strategies and tactics. It is a skill every entrepreneur should learn and apply in various complex situations of enterprise management. It helps the entrepreneur to build positive and genuine relationships with individuals in the entrepreneurial ecosystem.

Entrepreneurs want to build confidence among employees regarding the vision and goals of the enterprise. Communication skills help the entrepreneur

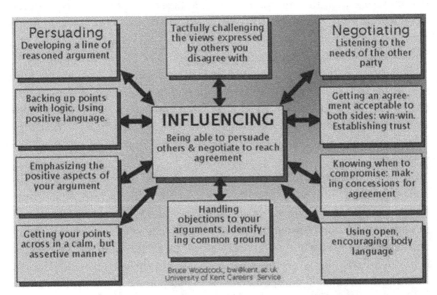

Figure 3.1 *Influencing Source*: Bruce Woodcock, bw@kent.ac.uk, University of Kent Careers Service.

establish strong relationships with stakeholders and clients. By adopting different communication channels and strategies, the entrepreneur succeeds in introducing fast, positive changes to the organization. It helps the entrepreneur to negotiate and sign contracts with external stakeholders in the interest and growth of the entrepreneurial venture. Good communication skills motivate and encourage employees and promote creativity and innovation in the organization (Samira, 2019).

An entrepreneur's successful performance is highly dependent on how the stakeholders respond to the decisions made by the entrepreneur in the context of the entrepreneurial venture. More often than not, the entrepreneur finds it difficult to convince other stakeholders such as employees, investors and suppliers about the decisions made. It is not possible to make everyone happy all the time. Through effective negotiation planning, strategies and tactics, the entrepreneur can influence other stakeholders in a deadlock or an impasse.

An entrepreneur should remember to focus on the purpose of communication in negotiation. Understanding the objectives, priorities and focus of negotiation will help the entrepreneur to communicate effectively during negotiations. Paying attention to how the entrepreneur delivers the messages while communicating with the opponent makes a difference in the outcomes of negotiation. Also important is the body language of the entrepreneur, such as facial expressions, hand movements, body postures and eye contact. To communicate well, the entrepreneur should observe and keep pace with the opponent in terms of the speed of talk, serious with respect being paid to/by the counterpart. This enables the negotiation to move easier as it provides equal status and respect for both parties involved.

Persuasion skills play an important role in a negotiator's dialogue with the opponent. Important persuasive techniques, such as asking the opponent to first present their viewpoint, patient listening and asking questions, offering concessions, delaying and not hurrying to concede to the other party, high level of patience displayed by the negotiator can change the outcome of the negotiation.

To achieve successful outcomes in negotiation, the entrepreneur must enhance his/her influencing skills. The unique skills inspire others indirectly. It is the true "buy-in" from different stakeholders that is important in entrepreneurship. An entrepreneur needs to strive to cultivate the influencing skills to garner attention and support from stakeholders. This would help in realizing the larger purpose and vision of the enterprise and would enhance the impact of entrepreneurial leadership across the board, ushering in the growth and development of the enterprise and the entrepreneurial ecosystem.

Key Terms

- Body language
- Communication
- Conflict management
- Entrepreneur
- Influencing skills
- Negotiation skills
- Non-verbal communication
- Persuasion skills
- Verbal communication

Review Questions

Q.1 What do you understand by the term "communication" in conflict management? Give one example of a situation wherein you came into conflict with a friend or family member due to the lack of proper communication.

Q.2 Based on the chapter, discuss some of the areas of entrepreneurship where an entrepreneur negotiates effectively with their counterparts. Select an entrepreneur of an enterprise based in your city who negotiated well in the past and secured the interests of the enterprise.

Q.3 "Learning the key tactics of communication helps the entrepreneur become a good negotiator." Make your arguments by citing a real example.

Q.4 How do you think the body language of an individual or opponent plays a significant role in negotiation? Discuss.

Q.5 Discuss the key aspects of persuasion skills that can help the negotiator to win a complex negotiation. Write a blog on persuasion skills and its role in negotiation for an entrepreneur in an e-commerce business.

Q.6 How do influencing skills become instrumental in effective negotiation? Conduct an interview with an entrepreneur who successfully applied the influencing skills in negotiation in the past, as part of his entrepreneurial interests or goals.

You Be the Entrepreneur

Passion and zeal for football can be seen, globally. Today, several teams are playing international football tournaments around the world. Players in international football have excellent opportunities to have a bright career in a short period which includes huge media attention, love and affection of fans from around the world, and a lot of opportunities to make money. One of the globally renowned leagues is the Ace League.

Ace League teams were to be selected for the upcoming tournament after a trade deal with Juventus I.P., Galatasaray O.C. and Monaco Pride fell through. The ultimate objective of the negotiation for Galatasaray was to hire a veteran player, Luis Puol. At present, Puol plays for Monaco. To ensure the deal does not occur, Galatasaray and Monaco brought in Juventus. Galatasaray and Juventus proposed several good players in exchange for Puol. To make the deal attractive, Galatasaray offered good players, Gerard Villa and David Harnandez. Hugo Coman and Miles from Juventus in the proposed list.

Interestingly in the last sentence, the name Miles is not a typo error. Monaco has two players with the last name Miles, David Miles, a 23-year-old center forward, and Jonty Miles, a 27-year-old right midfield. Somehow, Galatasaray and Juventus thought that David Miles was part of the deal, but Monaco was offering Jonty Miles. Surprisingly, no one clarified which Miles until the deal was almost confirmed.

When the teams found that they were looking at two different Miles, the deal came to a standstill and finally broke down. The news spread across social media. Some of the players had already indicated their formal selection. Meanwhile, several internal stories leaked and were debated widely in the press. In no time, the failure to make the deal due to such a communication gap brought an embarrassment to the teams' owners, association and players. Eventually, David Miles was traded to Galatasaray. The big embarrassment, effect on personal brands and tension in the locker room could have been averted by using the right channel of communication.

Miscommunication cannot be completely avoided and is always a part of negotiation. While no communication is guaranteed to be perfect, communication gaps, mistakes and misinterpretations can be caught early by being meticulous. One can make sure not to repeat such embarrassments in future negotiations. The concerned members need to confirm what has been expressed to them or their counterparts, and how it has been understood and absorbed by the members about an issue of negotiation.

Source: "A tale of two Brooks: the importance of communication in negotiation" by Megan Winkeler, December 2016 www.mwi.org

Case

Steve Fernandes has been working in the software industry in Silicon Valley, California, for 25 years. He was looking for early retirement as he wanted to spend the rest of his life in a peaceful place, far away from the hustle-bustle of a big city. He decided to settle down in Vernon, the smallest town in

California. Steve and his wife were quite happy with the new plan to reside in Vernon. However, they wanted to build their own house before they moved to a small town. Steve preferred to buy a plot of land first on which to build a house. He was aware of a half-hectare plot for sale for nearly three years. The owner was trying to sell the plot with the help of two local real estate agencies.

Steve found a new "for-sale" advertisement in the local daily. The new plot mentioned in the advertisement was the same as what he had been seeing over the last three years on the internet. The price of the new plot was $2,500,000. The price was higher by $20,000, in comparison to the previous price quoted by the two real estate agencies in the past. Steve wondered since the owner could not sell the plot at a lower price in the last three years, why would he raise the price to $2,500,000 despite knowing that he failed to sell the plot at a lower price in the past.

To collect more information about the plot, Steve decided to inquire at the Mayor's office. He wanted to confirm that there were no legal restrictions in planning construction. He also checked detailed information regarding the policies and guidelines for the construction of a building on this construction site. Steve felt good knowing the plot was free from any such planning restrictions. The advertisement on the internet carried the name and information of the contact person for all queries related to the sale of the plot. The contact person was referred to as the "selling agent" in the advertisement. Ms Veronica was the name mentioned as the selling agent for the plot.

The next day, Steve met Ms Veronica regarding his interest in buying the plot. Ms Veronica claimed that several potential buyers were also showing interest in buying the plot. She stated that the potential buyers are even from other locations. She informed Steve that the plot was owned by George Bendell from Las Vegas where he currently lived. He was old and could not travel long distances. Ms Veronica stressed the price of $2,500,000 was quoted by Bendell, the owner. She conveyed that the owner was determined to get the selling price as he was not in a hurry to close the deal. Essentially, the selling agent told Steve that the owner insisted on the negotiations regarding the selling of the plot needed to take place through the selling agent.

Having reviewed the situation, Steve felt that the bargaining power of the owner was strong, and he was determined to sell the plot at the increased selling price of $2,500,000. The stubborn nature of Ms Veronica could be due to her large commission if the deal closes. The owner might have left the task of selling the plot to the selling agent. He might have had the belief that the commission attached to the deal could strongly motivate the selling agent, Ms Veronica, to work hard and close the deal.

Given the complex situation, Steve was pondering about the possible ways to negotiate. Some of the questions in his mind were: was the selling price of $2,500,000 worth the plot of land? Should he go over it the asking price? Should he consider quoting a price that was less than the current selling price? What should be his actual buying price? Steve's challenge was he did not have sufficient money to buy at the selling price of $2,500,000.

Steve was also concerned about other aspects of buying the plot. He found the plot was not ready for the construction of a building. The major portion of the land required clearing of bush and overgrowth. The land was abandoned and completely neglected with trash being dumped there for many years. The plot required proper clearing, cleaning and landscaping. Leveling the ground and fencing would be required to protect from stray animals. A private access road of 600 meters would also be needed. Other expenses include fees for the services of an architect, installation fees for electricity, sanitation, sewage work and water requirements. To meet all these financial requirements, Steve would have to approach either banks or financers to avail home loans. As he was 47 years old, there could be approval issues with a home loan. He believed he would struggle financially to get his loans sanctioned.

Steve never wanted to have a mediating person. In this case, Ms Veronica, the selling agent was adamant to sell the plot and did not facilitate the meeting with the owner. Steve preferred to have direct negotiations with the owner, and he was not happy that the owner increased the selling price of the plot from $2,300,000 to $2,500,000, a straight jump of $20,000. Steve's financial options to buy the plot were limited and the expenses were significant. Examining the situation, Steve decided that he would not accept the increased selling price. The pressure mounted for Steve when he realized others might buy the plot if Steve delayed the negotiation with the selling agent, Ms Veronica, and indirectly with the owner.

Based on the chapter and the above-mentioned case, answer the following questions:

Q.1 Analyze the situation for possible negotiation from the perspective of a negotiator. How would you begin the negotiation in this case?

Q.2 Identify the major conflicting interests observed in the case between Steve and Ms Veronica/the owner, Bendell.

Q.3 Discuss some of the persuasion techniques that Steve must apply while negotiating with Ms Veronica/the owner, Bendell.

Q.4 Discuss the negotiation strategy and best alternatives Steve should have ready for the expected negotiation directly with the owner.

Q.5 Identify the possible negotiation outcomes if Steve had negotiation with Ms Veronica and the owner, Bendell, separately. What influencing tactics could be effective for Steve to negotiate strongly with each?

Suggested Readings

1. Interpersonal skills for entrepreneurs

Contreras Melissa (2013). Interpersonal Skills for Entrepreneurs, bookboon.com

Business leaders inspire others to take positive action in their ventures. To succeed at this, they learn to master their interpersonal skills. This book aims to help improve the way people relate to others in order to cultivate a reputation as a reliable partner, trustworthy boss or credible business professional.

2. Does communication skills matter to a nascent entrepreneur?

Abd Rani S.H., Migiro S.O., Adeyeye O.P., & Odewale G.T. (2019). Does communication skills matter to a nascent entrepreneur? Journal of Contemporary Management, 16(1), 209–225.

The article evaluates the relevance of entrepreneurship education in communication skills in developing nascent entrepreneurs. Attention is given to nascent entrepreneurs, the role of entrepreneurship education and issues of entrepreneurship; this leads to the significance of communication skills. This study indicates an imperceptible place of communication skills in the entrepreneurship domain.

3. Significance of entrepreneurs negotiation and communication skills

Slogar, Helena.Economic and Social Development: Book of Proceedings; Varazdin: 583-587. Varazdin: Varazdin Development and Entrepreneurship Agency (VADEA). (Apr 10–Apr 11, 2014)

This paper highlights the fundamental hypothesis of the importance of the development of entrepreneur communication skills in the negotiation process as a key competence in the development of entrepreneurship. The purpose of this paper is to raise awareness among entrepreneurs of the importance that knowledge of negotiating tactics has for those who steer business processes as well as for the implementation of common principles of communication, acceptance and cooperation in the business environment.

References

Bazerman, M. H., and Carroll, J. S. (1987). 'Negotiator cognition'. In L. L. Cummings and B. M. Staw (Eds.), *Research in Organizational Behavior*, Vol. 9, pp. 247–288. Greenwich, CT: JAI Press.

Bazerman, M. H., and Neale, M. A. (1983). 'Heuristics in negotiation: Limitations to effective dispute resolution'. In M. Bazerman and R. Lewicki (Eds.), *Negotiation in Organizations*, pp. 51–67. Beverly Hills: Sage.

Blickle, G. (2003). 'Convergence of agents' and targets' reports on intraorganizational influence attempts'. *European Journal of Psychological Assessment*, Vol. 19, No. 1, pp. 40–53.

Blickle, G. (2004). 'Einflusskompetenz in organisationen'. *Psychologische Rundschau*, Vol. 55, No. 2, pp. 82–93.

Chen, I. S., and Tseng, F.-T. (2016). 'The relevance of communication media in conflict contexts and their effectiveness: A negotiation experiment'. *Computers in Human Behavior*, Vol. 59, pp. 134–141.

Cialdini, R. B. (2007). 'Influence: The psychology of persuasion'. pp. 21–29.

Conger, J. A. (1998), 'The necessary art of persuasion'. *Harvard Business Review*, Vol. 76, No. 3, pp. 84–95.

Curran, J. (2020). 'The difference between negotiation and persuasion?'. https://www .huthwaiteinternational.com/horizons/the-difference-between-persuasion-and -negotiation (Accessed 10 June 2020).

Fisher, R., and Ury, W. (1981). *Getting to Yes: Negotiating Agreement Without Giving In*. Boston: Houghton Mifflin.

Galin, A., Gross, M., and Gosalker, G. (2007). 'E-negotiation versus face-to-face negotiation what has changed – If anything?' *Computers in Human Behavior*, Vol. 23, No. 1, pp. 787–797.

Geiger, I., and Parlamis, J. (2014). 'Is there more to email negotiation than email? The role of email affinity'. *Computers in Human Behavior*, Vol. 32, No. 1, pp. 67–78.

Hollingshead, A. B., McGrath, J. E., and O'Connor, K. M. (1993), 'Group task performance and communication technology: A longitudinal study of computer-mediated versus face-to-face work groups'. *Small Group Research*, Vol. 24, No. 3, pp. 307–333.

Kelley, H. H., and Thibaut, J. W. (1978). *Interpersonal Relations: A Theory of Interdependence*. New York: Wiley.

Kelman, H. C. (1958). 'Compliance, identification, and internalization three processes of attitude change'. *Journal of Conflict Resolution*, Vol. 2, No. 1, pp. 51–60.

Kipnis, D., and Schmidt, S. M. (1988). 'Upward-influence styles: Relationship with performance evaluations, salary, and stress'. *Administrative Science Quarterly*, Vol. 33, No. 4, pp. 528–542.

Kipnis, D., Schmidt, S. M., and Wilkinson, I. (1980), 'Intraorganizational influence tactics: Explorations in getting one's way'. *Journal of Applied Psychology*, Vol. 65, No. 4, pp. 440–452.

Lee, S., Han, S., Cheong, M., Kim, S. L., and Yun, S. (2017). 'How do I get my way? A meta-analytic review of research on influence tactics'. *The Leadership Quarterly*, Vol. 28, No. 1, pp. 210–228.

Lewicki, R. J., Barry, B., and Saunders, D. M. (2010). *Negotiation*, 6th ed. New York, NY: McGraw-Hill.

Loewenstein, J., Morris, M. W., Chakravarti, A., Thompson, L., and Kopelman, S. (2005), 'At a loss for words: Dominating the conversation and the outcome in negotiation as a function of intricate arguments and communication media'. *Organizational Behavior and Human Decision Processes*, Vol. 98, No. 1, pp. 28–38.

Pruitt, D. G. (1981). *Negotiation Behavior*. Orlando, FL: Academic Press.

Pruitt, D. G. (1983). 'Integrative agreements: Nature and antecedents'. In M. H. Bazerman and R. J. Lewicki (Eds.), *Negotiating in Organizations*, pp. 35–50. Beverly Hills, CA: Sage.

Purdy, J. M., Nye, P., and Balakrishnan, P. V. (2000). 'The impact of communication media on negotiation outcomes'. *International Journal of Conflict Management*, Vol. 11, No. 2, pp. 162–187.

Rackham, N., and Carlisle, J. (1978a). 'The effective negotiator, part 1: The behaviour of effective negotiators'. *Journal of European Industrial Training*, Vol. 2, No. 6, pp. 6–10.

Rackham, N., and Carlisle, J. (1978b). 'The effective negotiator, part 2: Planning for negotiations'. *Journal of European Industrial Training*, Vol. 2, No. 7, pp. 2–5.

Samira, G. (2019). 'The role of effective communication in entrepreneurial success'. https://www.entrepreneur.com/article/336347 (Accessed 28 May 2020).

Sheffield, J. (1995). 'The effect of communication medium on negotiation performance'. *Group Decision and Negotiation*, Vol. 4, No. 2, pp. 159–179.

Walker, T. J. (2011). 'Why Steve jobs was the ultimate communicator'. https://www.forbes.com/sites/tjwalker/2011/10/06/why-steve-jobs-was-the-ultimate-communicator/#128d47d35a5e (Accessed 28 May 2020).

Yukl, G. A. (2013). *Leadership in Organizations*, 8th ed. Boston, MA: Pearson.

Yukl, G. A., Guinan, P. J., and Soitolano, D. (1995). 'Influence tactics used for different objectives with subordinates, peers, and superiors'. *Group & Organization Management*, Vol. 20, No. 3, pp. 272–296.

Yukl, G. A., and Tracey, J. B. (1992). 'Consequences of influence tactics used with subordinates, peers, and the boss'. *Journal of Applied Psychology*, Vol. 77, No. 4, pp. 525–535.

PART II

ENTREPRENEURSHIP: MINIMIZE MISTAKES TO MAXIMIZE GAINS

Chapter 4

INTRAPERSONAL AND INTERPERSONAL DYNAMICS IN ENTREPRENEURSHIP

Learning Objectives

1. To understand the interconnectedness between psychology and entrepreneurship
2. To introduce different cognitive biases confronted by an entrepreneur
3. To learn about different types of personalities and attitudes of entrepreneurs
4. To familiarize with different sets of emotions of an entrepreneur
5. To recognize the role of an entrepreneurial mind-set, and how it becomes a differentiating factor for an entrepreneur

Opening Scenario: **Apple and US Book Publishers**

The US Department of Justice (DOJ) sued Apple and five major US publishers for colluding to raise the prices of ebooks. Three of the publishers settled the suit; two others and Apple were unwilling to settle.

The publishers had negotiated a new business model for ebook pricing with Apple as it prepared to launch the iPad: in exchange for a 30 percent sales commission, Apple would let the publishers set their own prices for ebooks. For the publishers, this pricing model appeared to be a vast improvement on their wholesaling arrangement with Amazon. After at least one of the publishers threatened to delay the release of its digital editions, Amazon reluctantly replaced its flat $9.99 price for ebooks with Apple's model, and prices rose industry-wide to about $14.99 on average.

The DOJ's lawsuit suggests that the negotiators and attorneys involved may have neglected to thoroughly analyze whether their agreement would truly create value for consumers and thus whether it fell within the parameters of US antitrust law. In the flush of hammering out a deal that appears to create synergy for everyone involved, negotiators sometimes neglect to consider how their agreement could affect outsiders, an oversight with ethical and legal implications.

Understanding Interconnections between Psychology and Entrepreneurship

Entrepreneurship has a multidisciplinary perspective. Disciplines such as psychology, economics, sociology and anthropology contributed to the development of the field of entrepreneurship during the last years. Psychology is one discipline that has had a strong influence on entrepreneurship. Essentially, psychological characteristics as demonstrated by the entrepreneur play an important role in entrepreneurship. Major scholars, such as Schumpeter (1934) and later McClelland (1967), have contributed to the psychological perspective particularly in terms of individuals and their behavior also; economic and strategic theories have been used to understand entrepreneurship (Kirchhoff, 1991). Research has also focused on the psychological perspectives of entrepreneurship to understand how individuals take decisive actions to move through an uncharted territory full of risks and uncertainties (Baum et al., 2007).

Baron (2007) posited entrepreneurship as a process. The process was divided into three stages. The first stage encompassed the identification of opportunities; in this stage, the entrepreneur explores and identifies feasible opportunities. In the second stage—the launch of the enterprise—the entrepreneur gathers resources to start the venture. In the third stage, the entrepreneur makes decisions related to the growth and scale-up of the enterprise. According to Hambrick (2007), psychological concepts play a significant role in all three stages of entrepreneurship. The first stage is predominantly influenced by the personality traits, attitudes and motivation of an entrepreneur. These elements of psychology affect the decisions of the entrepreneur in their entrepreneurial ventures.

In the later stages, by psychologically influencing others and by building a network, relationships and rapport with like-minded contributors, the entrepreneur gradually progresses in the building of the entrepreneurial venture in the long run. The involvement of other internal and external stakeholders intensifies stage two and stage three when the entrepreneurial venture grows. Essentially, leadership demonstrated by the entrepreneur is a critical influence and inspiration for all the stakeholders of the venture. Entrepreneurial leadership develops the trust and commitment needed for the success of the venture.

Understanding the psychological aspects of an entrepreneur is very relevant in today's competitive business environment. It is interesting how the mental structures facilitate an individual to interpret and comprehend new information in a given situation. Mitchell et al. (2007) posit that the psychological ability of an individual to interpret and comprehend any new information helps in the identification of entrepreneurial opportunities and unmet markets. The learning ability of an individual is a psychological process of observation, interpretation and comprehension. Learning by an individual leads to practical intelligence in terms of knowing and doing. Psychologically, both tacit knowledge and abilities strengthen the entrepreneur at the individual level, which in turn helps to deal with entrepreneurial challenges and activities (Baum & Bird, 2010). Factors driven by emotions, such as initiatives, passion, positive thinking and vision, have had significant research in recent years in the field of entrepreneurship (Cardon et al., 2012).

The psychological perspectives and concepts have a significant role to play in the success of an entrepreneur at both the individual and group levels.

Biases of Entrepreneurs in the Entrepreneurial Journey

Cognitive biases are very common. There is a cognitive phenomenon observed in every individual. Entrepreneurs are no different. Cognitive bias is understood better when it is separated from the rationality in judgment. Then a typical pattern emerges at least for a definite period of time. The pattern lacks logical reasoning and supported argument. When an individual is affected by cognitive biases in a given situation, they live in a subjective environment due to the perceived differences and available inputs. It is a perceived reality, not the actual reality.

Cognitive biases are constructed based on the processed information. Any distortion or slight deviation from the reality makes the individual perceive the situation, person or event differently. Each individual brings their own perceived notions about the issue to the table, and the differences among people surge. Our past experiences, expectations of others, social taboos, pressures, belief systems, emotional conditions and level of satisfaction influence our decision-making abilities while information processing occurs. Cognitive biases influence the decision making of an individual either positively or negatively. Ineffectiveness of the outcomes results from the decision-making process.

When establishing and running their enterprises, entrepreneurs deal with the cognitive biases in all stages of entrepreneurship. Some solid decision making is critical for an entrepreneur; any type of cognitive biases may be harmful to the enterprise and its future by affecting the small and large decisions made by the entrepreneur over a period of time. Research has shown how cognitive biases can be a serious threat to the existence of any entrepreneurial venture. Cognitive biases influence all the decisions in the long run. It affects the brand value and impression of the customers due to biased decisions made by the entrepreneur.

Entrepreneurs are the founders who start, scale and grow their enterprises with their entrepreneurial leadership. They have to deal with unprecedented challenges, responsibilities and commitment toward their internal and external stakeholders. Most of the time, the entrepreneur functions in a complex environment. The environment calls for risk-oriented behavior by the entrepreneur. It requires swift, unbiased and result-oriented decisions in the interest of all the employees who work for the enterprise and its growth in the long run. Under such a highly demanding environment, the entrepreneurs get more vulnerable to cognitive biases as they deal with stakeholders. Research posits that entrepreneurs tend to follow their hunches and gut feeling as part of their decision-making process. The golden rule for an entrepreneur is to be acquainted with the different cognitive biases while working at both the individual and group level within the entrepreneurial ecosystem.

Some of the major cognitive biases of the entrepreneur include hindsight bias, planning fallacy, confirmation bias, overconfidence bias, sunk cost fallacy, status quo bias and optimism bias.

Hindsight bias is common and assumes situations are based on one's own inclination toward past occurrences and experiences. It is known as "I-knew-it-all-along" effect. Hindsight-biased entrepreneurs assume that a particular condition that occurred in a particular manner in the past is going to occur again in the same manner. Hindsight bias makes the entrepreneur rely on false and illogical assumptions and, later, regrets the poor results or outcomes that occur. Entrepreneurs should not predict anything based on how a particular situation occurred in the past. Instead, they should evaluate the pros and cons of the situation to make the decisions that are in the interest of all the stakeholders of the enterprise.

Planning fallacy is a cognitive bias that occurs when the entrepreneurs choose to plan for the future without taking into consideration the major factors needed to attain different milestones in the entrepreneurial journey. The entrepreneur underestimates the costs needed, resources required and time available for the enterprise to start the new venture and continue growing the enterprise. The impact of poor decisions negatively affects the health of the entrepreneurial venture.

Overconfidence bias is the subjective confidence often witnessed in the life of entrepreneurs at different levels of industry growth. It is expected that every entrepreneur works full of confidence and performs in the best interests of the enterprise. However, overconfidence is always dangerous, especially when the entrepreneur is expected to collaborate, build teamwork and work for the common, larger interests of the stakeholders. It is necessary to understand one's own limitations in the context of what an entrepreneur is capable of doing, and not doing, in a given situation. An entrepreneur may think of sharing the responsibilities or tasks requiring special skills or expertise with those colleagues, partners, industry experts and specialists who carry the needed background.

Confirmation bias is also a common cognitive bias observed in entrepreneurs. It entails relating a present issue, event or situation and attempting to map it with a similar incident, issue or situation in the past. The entrepreneur tries to fit all the present ideas based on the preconceived notions. An entrepreneur having confirmation bias unknowingly tends to look only for information related to an issue, event or situation which relates to one's own past. Confirmation biases can be avoided by adequately analyzing all the factors which affected the past situations of the entrepreneur.

Sunk cost fallacy is another cognitive bias some entrepreneurs grapple with in their entrepreneurial journey. It is always good to have a strong desire, drive and passion in the pursuit of entrepreneurial goals, targets and objectives. This "never say die" attitude certainly enables the entrepreneur to keep trying until success is achieved. However, in many cases, the entrepreneur chooses to invest unreasonable time, overspend limited money and consume all the limited resources without any visible gain. The entrepreneur ignores the various limitations in the entrepreneurial process. This cognitive bias is called the sunk cost fallacy. The best way to deal with the sunk cost bias is to first admit that success does not mean to constantly chase the dream, ignoring other indicators or cues. Paying heed to such indicators or cues helps in either curbing the irrational and unnecessary efforts or pivoting to an alternate strategy.

Status quo bias makes the entrepreneur maintain the present conditions intact without making any changes to the status quo. Research has confirmed status quo bias in entrepreneurs. It reflects fear in the mind of an entrepreneur and limits the entrepreneur in making unbiased decision. To remove this bias, the entrepreneur must evaluate the current situation by taking into consideration all the feats and looking for a better option.

Optimism bias is related to the idea "that will never happen to me." Entrepreneurs often grapple with optimism bias. They downplay factors, situations and events working against them. They fail to estimate or measure the impact of both the internal and external factors and conditions. This results in poor judgment and bad decisions. An entrepreneur can become overly confident and makes irrational decisions ignoring valuable suggestions from others. The solution to eliminate this bias is to first admit that the entrepreneur is not free from the impact of environmental forces. All stakeholders, including the entrepreneur, are bound to get affected by the micro and macro conditions of the entrepreneurial ecosystem. Preparation and readiness to change are the best options for an entrepreneur in any adverse situation.

All these biases have a significant impact on the decision making and negotiating abilities of an entrepreneur. Knowing about different cognitive biases helps the entrepreneur better understand his/her mind-set. Psychology also helps understand how cognitive biases affect the relationship of the entrepreneur with partners, colleagues, fellow workers and external stakeholders. It enables the entrepreneur to successfully navigate the entrepreneurial venture in collaboration with others by reducing and controlling the cognitive biases affecting major business decisions.

The relationship and impact of cognitive bias and entrepreneurial intention are indicated in figure 4.1. The figure also shows other elements of the relationship between optimism and overconfidence, as previously discussed, in terms of positive and negative entrepreneurial emotion and entrepreneurship intention.

Personality Types and Attitudinal Differences

Due to various factors, enterprises often collapse and succumb to the market forces. The real entrepreneur keeps trying and fighting back against the odds. Some entrepreneurs fail and some succeed in the entrepreneurial journey. The question of why some entrepreneurs fail and why others succeed is an area of research focus. It is of interest to know that the individuals who continue running their traditional businesses earn more (Hamilton, 2000). In recent times, entrepreneurship research focused on understanding the role of non-cognitive skills, especially personality and attitudes toward risks influenced entrepreneurs' decision making and judgments. Attempts have been made to understand the personality differences and attitudes of individuals.

Based on the studies to understand personality and attitudinal differences, some significant models and frameworks have been developed: Big Five Model, locus of control, need for achievement model, self-efficacy and innovativeness. Research has focused on risk attitudes, goals and aspirations of entrepreneurs as well.

The Big Five Model is about five different types of personality traits: openness to new experiences, extraversion, neuroticism, conscientiousness and agreeableness. Research shows that openness to new experiences is the most significant personality trait driving the new entrepreneurs at the early stage of their ventures. Openness to new experiences was followed by the personality traits Agreeableness and Extraversion as positively affecting individuals in becoming an entrepreneur.

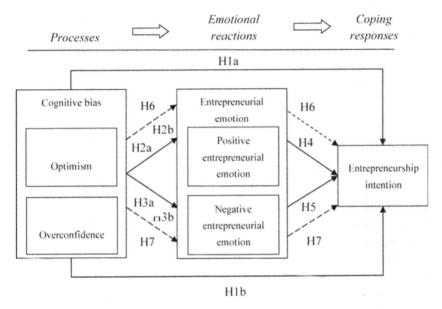

Figure 4.1 Relationship between cognitive bias and entrepreneurship intention. *Source*: https://www.frontiersin.org/articles/10.3389/fpsyg.2020.00625/full, Front. Psychol., 29 April 2020, https://doi.org/10.3389/fpsyg.2020.00625

Locus of control (LOC) is an important personality trait of the entrepreneur. LOC is focused either internally or externally. An individual whose LOC is internal makes his/her own decisions without depending on others. They maintain good control over their lifestyle, profession and family. They believe that they can influence the expected outcome through their own ability and skills. Individuals whose LOC is externally focused believe that destiny, chance, fate or the external factors in the environment influence outcomes. LOC was mentioned for the first time in the 1950s as part of the published works of Rotter (1954). While entrepreneurs embark on their entrepreneurial journey, it has been observed that they get influenced by the internal LOC as part of their personality traits (Shapero, 1975; Brockhaus, 1982; Gartner, 1985; Perry, 1990; Shaver & Scott, 1991). Internal LOC enables the entrepreneur to control or at least influence different factors in the environment and perform well in an entrepreneurial journey.

The personality trait—need for achievement—is important for the success of any entrepreneur. The need for achievement helps the entrepreneur remain focused and motivated to work tirelessly for the achievement of the objectives and goals. It is a strong desire to have accomplishments in an entrepreneurial journey through the right skillsets and attitude. An entrepreneur is better able to nurture the personality trait of the need for achievement in a relatively independent environment than an employee working under the superiors in an office with rules, regulations, strictness, authority and hierarchy. Need for achievement was first introduced by Murray (1938) and understood through the research of McClelland (1985) on "acquired needs theory." A study conducted by Stewart and Roth (2007) found that entrepreneur demonstrates a higher level of achievement than managers regardless of country.

Self-efficacy is also relevant in enabling an individual to become an entrepreneur. It is a strong belief in oneself to perform the tasks well and meet the expectations and targets (Cassar & Friedman, 2009). When an individual attains the target and higher performance in the workplace, self-efficacy has been found to be high (Stajkovic & Luthans, 1998). Increased growth and better academic performance reflect higher self-efficacy (Baum & Locke, 2004; Hacket & Betz, 1989; Luszcynska et al., 2005; Lent & Hackett, 1987).

Innovativeness is an important personality trait of an entrepreneur. According to Goldsmith and Foxall (2003), it is about how one responds to the unknown and unfamiliar, new conditions and situations. Hurt et al. (1977) in their study stated that measurement of innovativeness is very important. Researchers have found different ways to measure innovativeness since the early 1970s. An entrepreneur is an individual with an innovative mind to assess the environment.

Several studies confirm the attitudinal differences of the entrepreneur in terms of risk-taking capacity compared to a manager in the same industry. Early researchers, such as Knight (1921), proposed that entrepreneurs can be distinguished by their astuteness to perceive and grab opportunities without any fear of risk taking and uncertainties. A theory model was developed in the 1970s to predict the attitudes of individuals. It was used to determine that attitudes of individuals who are risk-averse would end up becoming employees after a while. The theory model also predicts the individual who becomes an entrepreneur is due in part to their risk-taking attitude (Khilstrom & Laffont, 1979).

The difference in the personality traits and attitudes plays a crucial role in enabling an entrepreneur to succeed or fail in his/her entrepreneurial journey. An individual who aspires to become an entrepreneur or serial entrepreneurs need to assess and check their personality traits and attitudes.

Role of Emotions: Should Entrepreneur Be an Emotional Being?

Several studies have confirmed that higher emotional intelligence (EI) leads to higher performance by an individual than a higher intelligence quotient (IQ). Entrepreneurs need to learn and nurture the ways to handle their emotions and those of others. Companies and entire industries are struggling across the world to manage the unprecedented economic conditions and change in the social fabric of the society. The paradigm shift in terms of digital transformation, online transactions, social media, technological advancements, emerging trends, crisis management, best practices and health preparedness have presented varied, unprecedented challenges and adverse conditions around the world. It affected both developed and emerging markets.

Entrepreneurs are no different than any other person when they are expected to be emotionally strong to deal with sensitive and delicate issues at the individual, group or higher level of the enterprise. Daniel Goleman popularized the term "emotional intelligence" in his 1996 book stating that EI is the capability to recognize one's own emotions in tandem with others' feelings and emotions. It is to understand each emotion at a deeper level and respond to others by being empathetic in approach. EI should guide the process of thinking and behavior of an individual to make better decisions while working with and for others in any given situation.

EI has five major components: self-awareness, self-regulation, internal motivation, empathy and social skills. As an entrepreneur, it is essential to understand the emotional dimension of human behavior. Often, emotions are not apparent when an individual communicates with others. The entrepreneur, while establishing contacts and networks with others, should learn to apply and practice the different aspects of EI to deal with other individuals effectively. The entrepreneur must not get carried away by both displayed and hidden emotions but should learn and apply EI represented by self-control, empathy, influence, awareness, self-confidence, achievement drive, transparency, adaptability, teamwork and collaboration in different situations.

An emotionally intelligent entrepreneur knows how to discuss with others and handle their emotions at an elevated stage. By being empathetic, the entrepreneur understands and feels the pain of the counterpart. Emotionally, they are not rigid and stubborn since EI helps them to accommodate the differences of opinions and disagreements with others as well as helps the entrepreneur be aware of their own strengths and weaknesses.

Entrepreneurial Mind-set for Entrepreneurial Behavior

Entrepreneurs are different in their thought process and the way they carry themselves. The statement "Mind-set is everything" became popularized in normal meetings, formal discussions and gatherings. Our mind-set can make us the best of a bad bunch or worst as well. It is the underlying mechanism of why and how we think about everything as an individual. Mind-set introduces or promotes us to explore great opportunities. It can also make us oblivious about the opportunities and cause us harm without being aware of the actual situation. An entrepreneur's success depends on the entrepreneurial mind-set they have from the early stage of their entrepreneurial journey.

Entrepreneurship is not easy. Numerous challenges, difficulties and dejections are all a part of any entrepreneurial venture. The entrepreneur is required to have a robust mind-set to tackle the challenges in an effective, smart way during the life span of the venture. Entrepreneurial mind-set significantly impacts the decisions made by the entrepreneur in the start and development of the venture. It also affects the other stakeholders of the enterprise positively or negatively. Entrepreneurs need to acknowledge the role of the entrepreneurial mind-set in the context of an entrepreneurial venture-start, growth and development.

Entrepreneurial mind-set is about one's own cognitive belief system. It consists of several interconnected beliefs, thoughts and assumptions which affect the entrepreneur in the decision-making process. The information is acquired and processed for a new set of entrepreneurial behavior which leads to a particular outcome related to the enterprise. Entrepreneurial mind-set encompasses a belief to succeed and attain the ownership of self. It helps in maintaining compelling goals, targets and plans achievement in a systematic order and approach. It drives an entrepreneur to have high resilience to deal with odd and adverse situations in his/her entrepreneurial journey. Entrepreneurial mind-set drives an entrepreneur to become a knowledge seeker by wanting to upgrade and advance their level of knowledge and develop curiosity, critical thinking, creativity and competence.

Entrepreneur with an entrepreneurial mind-set would carry a positive mental attitude, strong creative mind, capability to persuade others, be internally charged and motivated all the time, have perseverance to keep going and learn from failures and losses.

Chapter Summary

Entrepreneurship is the amalgamation of different factors, including the role of the entrepreneur, business ideas and opportunities, different systems and processes, business models, strategic management of the functional areas of marketing, finance, human resources and operations. One of the most significant factors which impacts entrepreneurship in any industry is the nature and individual characteristics of an entrepreneur. The individual characteristics of an entrepreneur are crucial to accomplish well-defined targets, goals and vision of an enterprise. The requirement is to better understand and analyze the psychological factors of an entrepreneur. An entrepreneur needs to understand the behavior of others and groups based on intrapersonal and interpersonal dynamics of those individuals.

Cognitive biases are one critical aspect that significantly impacts the way an entrepreneur operates in the entrepreneurial venture. Cognitive biases such as hindsight bias, planning fallacy, confirmation bias, overconfidence bias, sunk cost fallacy, status quo bias and optimism bias affect the decisions made by the entrepreneur. Cognitive biases distort the process of gathering, processing and interpreting the information from the environment. As a result, the quality of the decisions and judgments by the entrepreneur is compromised in terms of ineffective and poor outcomes. The poor decisions and judgments, in turn, negatively affect the survival and growth of the entrepreneurial venture in the long run.

Personality traits are one of the core attributes of an entrepreneur. These determine how effectively an entrepreneur understands his/herself in conjunction with other stakeholders and their expectations in the entrepreneurial journey. Attitudinal differences present in the entrepreneur also impact the future of the entrepreneurial venture. Successful entrepreneurs are not found to be risk-averse. They are enthusiastic and full of initiatives for the larger interests of the entrepreneurial venture. An entrepreneur needs to maintain a positive and "dare to win" attitude and respond to the actors and events affecting the situation. Emotions represented by thoughts, feelings, ideas and viewpoints are inevitable in any human interaction. Anger, sorrow, irritation, fear, happiness, anxiety, empathy and compassion are key emotions an entrepreneur experiences as part of the creation and growth of any enterprise. Fear of failure and loss is detrimental in the process of entrepreneurship. An entrepreneur cannot afford to thrive in the presence of fear. Fear affects an entrepreneur's decision-making capabilities and ability to analyze the situation accurately.

Having an entrepreneurial mind-set driven by passion is essential in today's erratic economic and social environment. Numerous factors may severely impact the operations and growth strategies of an entrepreneurial venture. Given the challenging situation, an entrepreneur must nurture a strong cognitive mechanism to understand and strengthen the process of thinking and, in turn, make balanced decisions in the larger interest of all the stakeholders of the enterprise.

Key Terms

- Attitudinal difference
- Cognitive biases
- Emotions

- Entrepreneurial mind-set
- Entrepreneurship
- Psychology
- Types of personality

Review Questions

Q.1 Discuss the interconnectivity or links between psychology and entrepreneurship. How do psychological aspects of an entrepreneur impact the functioning of an entrepreneur?

Q.2 Identify and write down the common cognitive biases of two close friends as observed by you. Each cognitive bias should be supported with a real-life example.

Q.3 "Every individual carries a certain type of personality." Based on this statement, discuss the major types of personalities mentioned in the chapter. What type of attitude do you think an entrepreneur requires to succeed in entrepreneurship?

Q.4 Based on the readings, should an entrepreneur be an emotional being in the entrepreneurial journey? Support with valid arguments.

Q.5 "Mind-set is everything." How deeply do you agree or disagree with the statement? What do you consider to be some of the possible ways to build an entrepreneurial mind-set?

You Be the Entrepreneur

Personality traits have a major role in the life of an entrepreneur. Several leaders and entrepreneurs in business have clearly demonstrated their unique and powerful personality traits. This helped them throughout their entrepreneurial journey working with other stakeholders. Some of the eminent entrepreneurs whose personality traits stand out are: Steve Jobs, Jeff Bezos, Sheryl Sandberg, Jack Ma and Warren Buffet.

Steve Jobs was an entrepreneur with an open-minded approach. He demonstrated this personality trait on several occasions while working with his employees. He made it possible for his employees to see what and how a personal computer changes the life of a person. Carrying the open-minded approach, Jobs was able to conceive the idea of introducing computers for personal work at home. He enabled his employees to be open-minded and believe in his vision to create a personal computer for the larger customer base across the global market. The rest is history.

We can take the example of Jeff Bezos, founder of Amazon. He always displayed the personality traits of being a focused individual throughout his career. From the early days of Amazon, he was convinced with the idea to remain focused on customer satisfaction and superior experience. He was extremely focused on spending every penny on customers. He always kept the costs under control as the company grew by leaps and bounds. In the case of Steve Jobs and Jeff Bezos, their personality traits, (open-minded and focused approach) helped them both become successful entrepreneurs.

The personality trait of Sheryl Sandberg has been very influential. In her early career, Sandberg would conduct meetings and presentations with her management team and subordinates. On one such occasion, she made an important announcement during a presentation. The announcement was not to use any PowerPoints in meetings. Her personality was so influential that her employees took her at her word and stopped using PowerPoints during client meetings. Later, when Sandberg joined Facebook, she was shocked to learn what had happened. She immediately decided to loosen the restrictions pertaining to the different tools available for Facebook employees during their presentations.

The next example of personality traits in an entrepreneur is willfulness. We can take the example of Jack Ma, founder of Alibaba. He demonstrated what it takes to get rejected for 30 odd jobs applied for before he successfully founded Alibaba in 1999. He admitted in several interviews that it was his willfulness that kept him going when the going got tough for him. In other words, it was his strong determination and perseverance that subsequently made him a billionaire.

Warren Buffet is known for his utmost modesty as one of his personality traits. We can cite an example from his personal life. He is one of the top 10 billionaires today. His total wealth is estimated to be more than 90 billion dollars. However, he still lives in a modest house that he purchased in Nebraska in 1958. The personality trait of being modest in his thinking and dealing with others has earned him respect and dignity all these years.

Source: "10 personality traits of legendary entrepreneurs" by Deep Patel, March 2018 www.entreppreneur.com

Case

John Moore in his childhood days would admire eminent entrepreneurs and their success stories. He also wanted to be a billionaire and an entrepreneur when he grew up. The desire made him start his first entrepreneurial venture when he was 19 years old. His first venture in the early 1990s was to run a sports magazine company. His target customers were college students and lower-level office managers and workers. To bring down the cost factor, he chose to outsource the work related to writing articles to freelancers and the copy editing and publishing of the magazine to a publishing house.

The publishing house belonged to his childhood friend, Samuel Gale. It was headquartered in Houston, Texas (USA). John chose to lead the sales and marketing of the product. When John started the magazine business, he was thrilled to set new trends in the publishing industry. Soon he realized it was not his passion. John chose to move out of the magazine business within three years. He felt he was ready to do something really big.

John met another entrepreneur, Linda Lawrence, who recently sold her startup to a big company. Linda was now ready to take up new projects. John met Linda at an international conference in New York. Both of them liked the personalities and attitudes of each other. They chose to start a new venture to educate school children by offering creative workshops. The biggest challenge was to negotiate with the school authorities and get them on board.

Several attempts were made to collaborate with schools. But the duo faced a lot of rejections from school authorities, especially in the way the workshops were designed for school children. John tried to convince Linda to entirely change the design of the workshops. She placed her own reasons to continue the design of the creative workshops. She suggested finding other potential clients who would be interested in the present design of the creative workshops.

John felt that Linda was not effectively putting effort in collaborating and accommodating the ideas and suggestions made by him. He felt his role getting smaller than Linda's. However, John decided to maintain the status quo and not break the collaboration with her. He chose to continue for more time hoping to see her understand his approach and appreciate his ideas. They used some of their contacts to secure a handful of creative workshops to be conducted for some of the schools. The growth was extremely slow. The business was not expanding.

John felt that Linda seemed to need to be an independent lady. She wanted to follow her own working style with less interference. Having been disappointed with Linda, John chose to cut out the relationship and look for better entrepreneurial opportunities. Without getting disheartened, John chose to continue to chase his own entrepreneurial dreams, he tried another 8–10 new business ideas. But he had his own individual and behavioral issues which led him to make poor decisions as an entrepreneur. As a result, none of his entrepreneurial ventures could succeed and they failed. Eventually, this affected John psychologically so much that he turned out to be an extremely negative person in terms of his thoughts and actions. He started presenting himself as a failed entrepreneur with no luck or money. In spite of having big dreams,

John Moore could not become a successful entrepreneur and failed to live up to his own expectations.

Based on the chapter and the above-mentioned case, answer the following questions:

Q.1 What do you understand by the personality of an individual? In your mind, what were the personality traits of John Moore?

Q.2 Explain cognitive biases. Discuss the cognitive biases observed in the case of John Moore.

Q.3 Was John Moore affected by bad luck, poor destiny or suffering from cognitive biases? Highlight the instances from the case to support your answer.

Q.4 If you were in the position of John Moore, how would you have handled the deteriorating relationship differently with the partner, Linda, specifically the joint venture of the creative workshop business for school children?

Suggested Readings

1. Surviving the emotional rollercoaster called entrepreneurship: The role of emotion regulation

De Cock, Robin & Denoo, Lien & Clarysse, Bart. (2019). Surviving the emotional rollercoaster called entrepreneurship: The role of emotion regulation. Journal of Business Venturing. 35. 10.1016/j.jbusvent.2019.04.004.

Entrepreneurs endure a variety of emotions during their journey as an entrepreneur. Emotion regulation is a significant mechanism that entrepreneurs utilize to cognitively appraise events and suppress their expression in response to their emotions in order to adapt to situations in their favor. The authors studied the relationship between habitual use of emotion regulation among entrepreneurs and the likelihood of survival of their ventures. Founders dealing with poorly performing ventures are more likely to recover if they suppress their emotions. Reappraising a problematic event repeatedly might lower the chances of bouncing back as the founder may deviate from problem-focused coping mechanism.

2. The entrepreneurial process: The link between intentions and behavior

Gieure, Clara & Benavides-ESpinosa, M Mar & Roig-Dobón, Salvador. (2020). The entrepreneurial process: The link between intentions and behavior. Journal of Business Research. 112. 10.1016/j.jbusres.2019.11.088.

The authors studied what enables the initiation of entrepreneurial intentions among students. The relationship between entrepreneurial intentions and behavior toward initiating a business was explored. It was asserted that the personal attitudes of students did not influence their intentions to start a business. The students develop attitude toward starting a business when they have the knowledge or capability to start a business. Students are more likely to initiate a business if they are aware of subjective norms of running a business which they might gain through enrolling in courses. Universities help students by generating the entrepreneurial drive by facilitating necessary resources.

3. The influence of personality traits and demographic factors on social entrepreneurship startup intentions

Nga, Joyce & Shamuganathan, Gomathi. (2010). The Influence of Personality Traits and Demographic Factors on Social Entrepreneurship Start Up Intentions. Journal of Business Ethics. 95. 259-282. 10.1007/s10551-009-0358-8.

The concept of social entrepreneurs has been studied in the paper. The authors have emphasized that the time is ripe for entrepreneurs to integrate social, economic and environmental values into business. The adoption and expansion of social entrepreneurship are dependent on the personality traits of entrepreneurs. Providing necessary education might enable the enhancement of such traits in prospective social entrepreneurs. Of the big five personality traits, agreeableness is one dimension that influences all dimensions of social entrepreneurship. The authors also assert that openness positively impacts social vision, innovation and financial returns.

4. The Yin and Yang of entrepreneurship: Gender differences in the importance of communal and agentic characteristics for entrepreneurs' subjective well-being and performance

Hmieleski, Keith & Sheppard, Leah. (2018). The Yin and Yang of entrepreneurship: Gender differences in the importance of communal and agentic characteristics for entrepreneurs' subjective well-being and performance. Journal of Business Venturing. 34. 10.1016/j.jbusvent.2018.06.006.

Gender differences play an important role in entrepreneurship. The authors have classified entrepreneurial characteristics into two broad categories: predominantly masculine and feminine. These characteristics interact with biological gender to generate subjective well-being among entrepreneurs and objective performance of venture firms. Based on the author's suggestions, creative women entrepreneurs and teamwork proficient male entrepreneurs perceive themselves as better suited for the work thereby leading to higher subjective well-being and venture performance.

5. Founder passion, neural engagement and informal investor interest in startup pitches: An fMRI study

Scott Shane, Will Drover, David Clingingsmith, Moran Cerf, Founder passion, neural engagement and informal investor interest in startup pitches: An fMRI study, Journal of Business Venturing, Volume 35, Issue 4, 2020, 105949, ISSN 0883-9026, https://doi.org/10.1016/j.jbusvent.2019.105949.

Emotional expressions displayed by entrepreneurs have a variety of impacts on their stakeholders. The affective state of passion is commonly exhibited by entrepreneurs. This study reveals the impact of expression of passion in entrepreneurial pitches on the informal interest among investors. The functional magnetic resonance imaging method was utilized to study the impact on the informal investors. In tune with intuition, expression of passion in the pitch of entrepreneurs positively impacted both investor neural engagement and investor interest in the venture by 39 percent and 26 percent, respectively. Investor neural engagement is in turn positively related to the investor interest in the startup being passionately promoted by the entrepreneur.

References

Baron, R. A. (2007). 'Behavioral and cognitive factors in entrepreneurship: Entrepreneurs as the active element in new venture creation'. *Strategic Entrepreneurship Journal*, Vol. 1, No. 1–2, pp. 167–182.

Baum JR, Bird BJ. (2010). 'The successful intelligence of high-growth entrepreneurs: Links to new venture growth'. *Organizational Science* 21(2):397–412.

Baum JR, Frese M, Baron RA, eds. (2007). *The Psychology of Entrepreneurship*. Mahwah, NJ: Erlbaum.

Baum JR, Locke EA. (2004). 'The relationship of entrepreneurial traits, skill, and motivation to new venture growth'. *Journal of Applied Psychology* 89(4):587–598.

Brockhaus RH. (1982). 'The psychology of the entrepreneur'. In CA Kent, DL Sexton, KH Vesper (eds.), *Encyclopedia of Entrepreneurship*. Englewood Cliffs, NJ: Prentice Hall, pp. 39–56.

Cardon MS, Foo M-D, Shepherd DA, Wiklund J. (2012). 'Exploring the heart: Entrepreneurial emotion is a hot topic'. *Entrepreneurship Theory & Practice* 36(1):1–10.

Cassar G, Friedman H. (2009). 'Does self-efficacy affect entrepreneurial investment?' *Strategic Entrepreneurship Journal* 3:241–260.

Gartner WB. (1985). 'A conceptual framework for describing the phenomenon of new venture creation'. *Academy of Management Review* 10:696–706.

Goldsmith RE, Foxall GR. (2003). 'The measurement of innovativeness'. In LV Shavinina (ed.), *The International Handbook of Innovation*. Oxford, UK: Elsevier Science, pp. 321–328.

Hackett G, Betz NE. (1989). 'An exploration of the mathematics self-efficacy/ mathematics performance correspondence'. *Journal for Research in Mathematics Education* 20(3):261–273.

Hambrick DC. (2007). 'Upper echelons theory: An update'. *Academy Management Review* 32(2):334–343.

Hamilton BH. (2000). 'Does entrepreneurship pay? An empirical analysis of the returns of self-employment'. *Journal of Political Economy* 108(3):604–631.

Hurt HT, Joseph K, Cook CD. (1977). 'Scale for the measurement of innovativeness'. *Human Communication Research* 4:58–65.

Khilstrom R, Laffont JJ. (1979). 'A general equilibrium entrepreneurial theory of firm formation based on risk aversion'. *Journal of Political Economy* 87:719–748.

Kirchhoff BA. (1991). 'Entrepreneurship's contribution to economics'. *Entrepreneurship Theory & Practice* 16(2):93–112.

Knight F. (1921). *Risk, Uncertainty, and Profit*. Boston, MA: Houghton Mifflin Co.

Lent RW, Hackett G. (1987). 'Career self-efficacy: Empirical status and future directions'. *Journal of Vocational Behavior* 30:347–382.

Luszczynska A, Scholz U, Schwarzer R. (2005). 'The general self-efficacy scale: Multicultural validation studies'. *The Journal of Psychology* 139(5):439–457.

McClelland DC. (1967). *The Achieving Society*. London: Free Press.

McClelland DC. (1985). *Human Motivation*. Glenview, IL: Scott Foresman.

Mitchell RK, Busenitz LW, Bird BJ, Gaglio CM, McMullen JS, et al. (2007). 'The central question in entrepreneurial cognition research'. *Entrepreneurship Theory & Practice* 31(1):1–27.

Murray HA. (1938). *Explorations in Personality*. Oxford, UK: Oxford University Press.

Perry C. (1990). 'After further sightings of the Heffalump'. *Journal of Managerial Psychology* 5:22–31.

Rotter JB. (1954). *Social Learning and Clinical Psychology*. Englewood Cliffs, NJ: Prentice Hall.

Schumpeter JA. (1934). *The Theory of Economic Development*. Cambridge, MA: Harvard Univ. Press.

Shapero A. (1975). 'The displaced, uncomfortable entrepreneur'. *Psychology Today*, pp. 83–88.

Shaver KG, Scott LR. (1991). 'Person, process, choice: The psychology of new venture creation'. *Entrepreneurship Theory and Practice* 16:23–45.

Stajkovic AD, Luthans F. (1998). 'Self-efficacy and work-related performance: A meta-analysis'. *Psychological Bulletin* 124(2):240–261.

Stewart WH, Roth PL. (2007). 'A meta-analysis of achievement motivation differences between entrepreneurs and managers'. *Journal of Small Business Management* 45(4):401–421.

Chapter 5

NEGOTIATION AND STARTUP VENTURES

Learning Objectives

1. Understand the importance of negotiation for startup ventures
2. Familiarize with historical developments of negotiation
3. Understand factors that impact the effectiveness of negotiation at individual and group levels
4. Understand the difference between integrative and distributive negotiation
5. Familiarize with outcomes of poor negotiation

Opening Scenario: Disney's Purchase of Lucasfilm

Walt Disney Company made a surprise announcement that it was acquiring Lucasfilm. Lucasfilm was founded by George Lucas who owned the famous Stars Wars brand. Walt Disney agreed to pay US$ 4.05 billion split evenly between stock and cash for the deal. Lucas was the sole shareholder of Lucasfilm.

The acquisition bolstered Disney's status as a leader in animation and superhero films. It was a beneficial deal for Disney as the company had rights to Star Wars and afforded them the opportunity to reap benefits from related merchandizing and media business. Disney promised to begin producing new Star Wars films every two to three years. The acquisition included a great deal of negotiation and even included a detailed script for three upcoming Stars Wars films.

The 68-year-old Lucas founded Stars Wars, and he had extensive negotiations with Disney before he settled for terms of purchase. After the purchase, it was agreed that Lucas will serve as a consultant for the acquired Star Wars brand. Lucas had been planning to retire for years. In a past interview with the *Times*, Lucas revealed that he was tired of the pressure of living up to the expectation of Star Wars fans.

According to Walt Disney Chairman Robert Iger, a famous negotiator in Hollywood, he and Lucas conducted the negotiations personally. Speaking of Lucas' decision to hand over his creative legacy to Disney, Igor told, "There was a lot of trust there." The acquisition of Star Wars by Disney illustrates the importance of building trust through successful negotiations when dealing with a powerful counterpart.

Startup Ventures and Negotiation

Startups are business ventures in their nascent stage and do not have a fully developed business models or other related strategic frameworks. Such ventures often lack funding and tend to rely on external funding to take their specialized products or services to market. An example of a startup is an accommodation rental website called Airbnb. The company was started in 2007 by three roommates in San Francisco who could not pay their rent, leading them to rent out air mattresses in their apartment (Aydin, 2020). The startup grew from its nascent stage and was worth US$ 31 billion by 2019.

To move a startup from its nascent stage to a more mature business, entrepreneurs must engage in negotiations with a variety of people, groups or organizations. Entrepreneurs also need effective negotiation skills when they wish to sell their ventures and exit a business. Negotiation is "a process through which two or more parties interact to create potential agreements intended to provide guidance and regulation to their future behavior" (Sawyer & Guetzkow, 1965). An entrepreneur behind a startup must engage in negotiation with potential employees, suppliers, future customers, regulatory authorities, potential investors over the duration of the entrepreneurial journey. Although there are many factors that define the success of a startup, negotiation skills and strategies adopted by the entrepreneur do have a significant impact on the success of startups. Please see figure 5.1 detailing various factors that have an impact on the outcome of negotiations between two parties. In this chapter, we will elaborate on various aspects of negotiation strategies and their implications on numerous outcomes in the context of startups.

Historical Background of Negotiation

Negotiation is an interesting behavior that impacts the outcomes of our dealings with other people and organizations. The word *negotiation* finds its roots in the French word *negociacion*. There are numerous cultures and languages across the world and each one of them has their own version of the concept known as negotiation. The Japanese call it "Kōshō," the Chinese call it "Tánpàn," Indians call it "baatacheet," Arabic speakers refer to it as

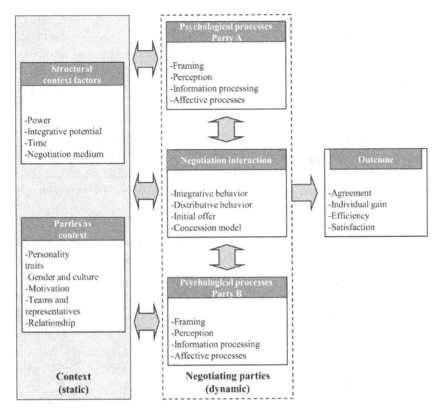

	Psychological processes Party A
Structural context factors	-Framing -Perception -Information processing -Affective processes
-Power -Integrative potential -Time -Negotiation medium	

| Negotiation interaction | Outcome |
| -Integrative behavior
-Distributive behavior
-Initial offer
-Concession model | -Agreement
-Individual gain
-Efficiency
-Satisfaction |

| Parties as context | Psychological processes Party B |
| -Personality traits
-Gender and culture
-Motivation
-Teams and representatives
-Relationship | -Framing
-Perception
-Information processing
-Affective processes |

Context (static)   **Negotiating parties (dynamic)**

Figure 5.1 Framework for behavioral negotiation theory. *Source*: Neale and Northcraft (1991: 177).

"tafawud," the Russians refer to it as "Peregovory." These are some examples of the omnipresence of the concept of negotiation in different parts of the world. No matter what the country, culture or language, negotiation in each of these countries has a lot in common. In almost all places, negotiation is associated with discussion and talks.

The association of negotiation with discussion and talks among people who are trying to reach an agreement leads us to think deeper about the evolutionary aspect of negotiation. Human beings are social creatures and have evolved phenomenal communication skills over thousands of years. There are variations among different countries in terms of languages, but at the end of the day human beings in different parts of the world have evolved to successfully communicate themselves and deliver their message. We as humans are no longer hunters and gatherers and live in proximity with each other. Living closely in towns and big cities has brought some unique challenges: the challenge to be able to protect self from deceptions and potential threats posed by other human beings and to strategize dealings with other humans maximizing personal gain (Dunbar et al., 1996). It is pretty evident that human beings do not perceive animals as threats to their safety, security and well-being anymore. Instead, the threats originate from other human beings.

An interesting question about negotiation is whether it is something that human beings have evolved and not present in other species. We for sure know that humans have evolved to develop cooperative rituals and behavioral patterns to alter outcomes of intra- and inter-group tensions or conflicts and prevent the threat and promote favorable outcomes; however, such behaviors are present in other species as well with the difference that other species use their unique cues, signals and behaviors innate to their own species (Darwin, 1913).

A key component of a successful negotiation is communication. Communication is "psychological and social interaction process through which two or more persons exchange current attitudes, emotions, and information to create better mutual understanding" (Varey et al., 2002). Communication can be verbal or written in nature. It is very important for entrepreneurs to have excellent communication skills when negotiating. Getting the right message to the right person is extremely critical to the success of any negotiation.

A legally binding form of communication is written communication. For entrepreneurs, deals and contracts with negotiating parties can be a form of written communication. When negotiators share opinions and information through written communication, it is termed as cognitive negotiation (Capes, 2013; Young et al., 2012). Historically cognitive negotiation has been an essential component of negotiation in the context of wars and treaties. Negotiation in conflicts happens when participants exchange cognitive and emotional information to reach a mutually acceptable solution that dissolves inconsistencies (Chen & Tseng, 2016).

Human beings have a long history of wars and conflicts that were eventually resolved by conflict negotiations. The outcome of negotiations is usually a treaty which is a mutually agreed upon resolution of future outcomes of expected behaviors. There is a long list of treaties in history with the oldest treaty named as Pact of Al-Hudaybiyah dating back to 628 AD and a more recent one being the 2009 Lisbon treaty (Britannica, 2021). Such treaties are a result of extensive negotiations between parties and usually avert future conflicts.

In the business world, treaties take the form of mergers and acquisitions. An example of a successful merger will be the US$ 26.5 billion merger deal between T-Mobile and Sprint in 2020 which made T-Mobile a stronger third largest mobile carrier in the United States (U.S News &World Report, 2020).

Entrepreneurs also engage in mergers and acquisitions, and the negotiations they engage in vary depending on the industry, location and size of the entrepreneur's business. In the following sections, we will discuss the importance of negotiation for entrepreneurs and how they can utilize successful negotiation strategies.

Negotiation at Individual, Departmental and Organizational Levels

Negotiation is an essential skill for any entrepreneur who engages in establishing startups. For any successful negotiation, it is essential to establish the agenda of negotiation before engaging in constructive communication with other parties. An agenda is primarily information about the issues to be brought to the table and structures of discussion through which the issues will be addressed by individuals and groups (Pruitt, 1983). When establishing agendas, the entrepreneur must keep in mind their relative power to other parties in negotiation as well as time constraints imposed by the nature of products and services carried by their business. Time constraints to initiate and complete negotiations are very critical for most businesses (Carnevale & Lawler, 1986). Not considering time constraints while establishing agendas can be detrimental to entrepreneurs as there is a high probability that higher time constraints will force the entrepreneur to settle for less and accept decisions that might not be favorable to the entrepreneurs' interests (Walton & McKersie, 1965). Such conditions are even more detrimental to the interests of startup entrepreneurs when they negotiate with individuals. Outcomes of negotiations with other individuals are impacted by the bargaining power of individuals on the other side of the negotiation table.

Power is "the power of A over B is equal to and based upon the dependence of B upon A." (Emerson, 1962: 33). When dealing with individuals, the perceived power of the entrepreneur is extremely critical. In the case of negotiations, such power can be conceptualized as bargaining power. Research suggests that people with higher bargaining power can extract more benefits for themselves than people with lower bargaining power (Walker, 1971). For example, let us assume that a gentleman named Tim establishes a technology startup named SoftSide systems. This is Tim's first foray in the technology sector and wishes to sell technology solutions to small businesses to automate inventory management. To be able to successfully build and sell the software, Tim needs to hire multiple software engineers who will create different versions of software for different industries. Also, Tim must contact different business owners and offer them customized software that best suits their needs. In this scenario, Tim has compromised bargaining power when he negotiates with the software developers as well as the business owners. The software developers know that Tim does not have much experience in software, and they would be more likely to charge him a premium for providing their services. Some developers may not even want to work for Tim as they may not view Tim's business as an opportunity for growth in their career. Thus, with compromised bargaining power, Tim must make sure that he familiarizes himself with the know-how of developing software and offer software developers career growth potential to avoid accepting outcomes of negotiations that might impact his interests negatively. While negotiating with businesses, Tim must make sure to conceal the age of his business and only focus on proposed savings for the business by adopting the software.

The dynamics of negotiation are a little different when a startup entrepreneur is negotiating with departments or organizations as such units have people negotiating on behalf of the entire unit. People negotiating on behalf of a business unit within a corporation have relatively lower personal interests vested in the deal. In such situations, the startup entrepreneur must gain trust and rapport among the negotiating parties. Perceived rapport between negotiating parties is positively related to building trust (Drolet & Morris, 1995). Rapport is "a close and harmonious relationship in which there is common understanding" (Oxford English Dictionary, 2005). Building rapport is essential for a startup entrepreneur because of the relative newness of startup. Startup entrepreneurs must keep in mind that it is their behavior that is essential in fostering rapport. We know that expressed behavior of negotiating parties fosters trust (Grahe & Sheman, 2007). The verbal behavior of negotiators is also key to building rapport in a negotiation setting (Bronstein et al., 2012).

It is not uncommon for startup entrepreneurs to negotiate with organizations in different geographical regions. Such variance in location brings along the challenge of cultural differences between the entrepreneur and the organization that they negotiate with. We know that human beings tend to favor people who are perceived to be like them (Brewer, 1986). The same principle comes into play in cases where entrepreneur tries to minimize the impact of cultural difference on negotiation outcomes. The entrepreneur must learn to develop cultural awareness by making sure they are tolerant of other's cultures, minimize cultural differences and be aware of the other's cultural characteristics. People who are tolerant of other people's cultures often exert effort to be sympathetic with cultural differences and disapprove of ethnocentrism (Kimmel, 1994). We also know that people who acknowledge cultural differences and view them as insignificant are more likely to be viewed as the ones who support cultural difference minimization (Bennet, 1986). It is very important for an entrepreneur to gain trust of the organization they work with by fostering trust through building rapport and minimizing cultural differences. While negotiating, entrepreneurs might be able to get more favorable outcomes for themselves if they enjoy the trust of people in the organizations they deal with.

Negotiation Styles in Startup Ventures

Entrepreneurs of startup ventures will encounter numerous situations where they will have to adapt their negotiation style to achieve the most favorable outcome for themselves. One such situation is where they approach potential customers, and the negotiation is about price of the product or service. In such cases, entrepreneurs can utilize the benefits of "the favor request effect." The favor request effect operates by influencing buyer's perceptions of the seller, wherein the buyer is made to believe that their interaction with seller is reciprocal and that they have received the lowest price (Blanchard et al., 2016). Under normal circumstances, buyers usually have the perception that the sole motivation of the seller is to make a financial benefit for themselves (Campbell & Kirmani, 2000). However, if the seller provides a small concession during negotiation, then the buyer will feel the need to reciprocate the concession (Maxwell et al., 2003). Such concessions could be discounts offered by the seller coupled with small requests for favors. The favors may not be repaid immediately but result in a desire to reciprocate among buyers (Burger et al., 1986). This effect is of great importance to startup entrepreneurs as they can utilize the effect to close deals faster and achieve better financial outcomes for themselves.

Like in any other negotiation scenario, startup entrepreneurs have key objectives which they wish to fulfill. Negotiators usually have the objective to maximize their personal economic gains while keeping the other negotiating parties satisfied (Graham et al., 1988). Negotiators must maintain the tricky balance of maximizing their personal gains as well as keeping the other negotiating party satisfied (Graham, 1986). One way to achieve this balance is by engaging in practice of "adaptive behavior." Adaptive behavior is the practice of altering one's negotiating style to better align with the negotiation style of other parties (Rubin & Brown, 1975). Research suggests that people who negotiate by engaging in adaptive behavior achieve better outcomes for themselves in negotiation settings (Weitz, 1978). The strategy of adaptive behavior can prove to be of great benefit to startup entrepreneurs.

Entrepreneurs like other negotiators have products or services to offer their clients. Such products and services have a price tag associated with them. In the context of business-to-business transactions, there is a possibility that the entrepreneurs will find themselves engaging in negotiations over the price of the product or service they offer. Some entrepreneurial negotiators engage in the strategy of offering a discount to potential customers. Such discounts give a very precise pricing estimate to the potential customer. But does providing precise prices do the entrepreneur any good? Research suggests otherwise. Yan and Pena-Marin (2017) suggested that offering prices in round numbers significantly increases the probability of the buyer accepting the offer. The authors have justified the phenomenon by claiming that people prefer round numbers as it symbolizes the completion of a deal. Thus, when negotiating prices it is in the best interest of entrepreneur to offer round prices instead of precise estimates to maximize the likelihood of buyer's acceptance of the offer.

Integrative vs Distributive Negotiation

A key feature of negotiation is the process where two or more parties interact and reach agreements which guide their future behavior (Sawyer & Getzkow, 1965). Negotiation is social activity among people of varying interests and completion of this activity requires cooperation among people (Thompson et al., 2010: 492). When people negotiate, they either engage in competitive or cooperative negotiation strategies. People who engage in competitive nego-tiation strategies have the desire to maximize their personal gains (De Dreu et al., 2000). Such desires lead people to opt for actions that can cause incon-clusiveness in decisions and outright refusal to accept offers from other parties in negotiation (Martin-Raugh, 2020). On the other hand, some negotiators engage in cooperative negotiation that focuses on maximizing gains for all the parties in negotiation (De Dreu et al., 2000). Negotiator adopting coop-erative strategies often engage in making compromises and have the tendency to make trade-offs that ultimately addresses high-priority issues while ignor-ing low-priority issues (Pruitt, 1983).

Distributive negotiation is based on the competitive negotiation strategy adopted by negotiators. Negotiators engaging in distributive negotiation have the sole desire to be the winner in negotiation and have little to no concern about the perceived benefits or well-being of other parties in negotiation pro-cess (Gelfand et al., 2011). Based on cooperative negotiation strategy, inte-grative negotiation is adopted by negotiators who believe in achieving joint gains for all parties and have the desire to look for solutions that enable ben-efits for all parties (Martin-Raugh, 2020). For entrepreneurs who represent startups, these two styles of negotiation will have a differential impact on the effectiveness of desired outcomes. There might be instances when startup entrepreneurs engage in negotiations with other parties and do not perceive long-term relationships with other parties. In such cases, the distributive negotiation is ideal. For example, an entrepreneur wants to purchase land for their manufacturing unit in a particular area. After careful search, the entrepreneur locates suitable land for sale and enters in a negotiation with the owners. In this case, the entrepreneur has no incentive to engage in integrative negotiation as the land purchase from the landowner is one-time activity and the possibility of purchasing land from the same owner is negligible. When the entrepreneur establishes manufacturing on that land and desires to hire labor for the factory, it is in the best interest of the entrepreneur to engage in integrative negotiation with potential factory workers. As the labor force is key to manufacturing, it is in the best interest of the entrepreneur to make sure that the interests of the labor force are addressed and honored right from the beginning of negotiations.

Impact of Poor Negotiation

So far, we have discussed numerous strategies that startup entrepreneurs can adopt to achieve maximum benefit from negotiations. However, what is equally important is to discuss what the entrepreneur should not do in negotiations. Poor negotiation can have a multitude of impact on the success of entrepreneurial ventures. Such impacts include loss of revenue, loss of trust among stakeholders, failure to capitalize on market potential and so on.

There are instances when negotiators engage in bad negotiation practice of false negotiation. False negotiation occurs when a negotiator has no desire to reach a decision and it is in their best interest to stall negotiation by delay tactics as it brings them higher financial gain (Glozman et al., 2015). Some negotiators stall the progress of negotiation and act as if they are cooperating with other parties toward the completion of the negotiation process while their goal is to never reach a conclusion. Research suggests that negotiators who engage in false negotiation are more likely to engage in behaviors such as repeating commitment to the process and emphasizing the importance of cooperation with other parties in negotiation (Glozman et al., 2015). How is false negotiation a bad strategy? False negotiation can be detrimental to the perceived trustworthiness of a startup venture and the entrepreneur. The negotiator engaging in false negotiation can delay the agreement for a particular period. After a certain period, the patience of other parties in negotiation will wear off and true intentions of the entrepreneurial negotiators will be revealed. Such instances might do unrepairable damage to the reputation and credibility of the entrepreneur.

Most negotiations have some level of information privacy between negotiating parties (Schweitzer & Hsee, 2002). Such private information enables the possibility of some negotiating party's engagement in private information misrepresentation to achieve personal gains (Koning et al., 2011). Such information misrepresentation is a type of deception. Deception is the activity where the deceiver intentionally misleads the deceived by misrepresentation of information and emotions (Gaspar et al., 2015). There are multitude of reasons why deception is bad and ultimately has less favorable outcomes. Although negotiators sometimes fail to detect deceptions (Lewicki & Hanke, 2012), they do perceive them as inappropriate when detected (Robinson et al., 2000) and have the tendency to punish the party who engaged in deception (Bornstein & Weisel, 2010). The implications of engaging in deception are extremely critical for startup entrepreneurs. As the startups are relatively newer and people do not have much information about the startup, the entrepreneur might be tempted to engage in deception by misrepresenting information about their startup. Such strategies might have a favorable outcome in the short run, but eventually the information asymmetry will most likely be resolved leading to revelations of deceptive intent of the entrepreneurs. In such cases, other negotiators are likely to punish the entrepreneur which might damage the reputation and credibility of the concerned entrepreneur.

While engaging in negotiations, people get carried away by their goals and do not put much emphasis on empathy. Empathy is an emotional response and involves actions motivated by compassion and care for others (Davis, 1983b). Lack of empathy in negotiation can have a detrimental impact on the outcome of negotiation. We know that empathy promotes cooperation (Batson & Ahmad, 2001) and discourages anti-social behavior (Miller & Eisenberg, 1988). Empathy also discourages immoral behavior among people (Batson et al., 2003). Such implications are critical for negotiations as entrepreneurs who are empathetic will achieve higher levels of cooperation from other negotiating parties. There is also the likelihood that empathetic entrepreneurs will not engage in immoral behavior which will in turn enhance their perceived trustworthiness. Thus, it is in the best interest of entrepreneurs to be empathetic toward other parties.

Chapter Summary

Negotiation for startup ventures is extremely important as entrepreneurs need favorable outcomes from negotiating parties. Such parties can be stakeholders such as employees, customers or even potential investors. Human beings tend to negotiate, and there are historical records of negotiations ending wars with formal treaties. In the business world such as for startup ventures, there are contracts instead of peace treaties.

Before entering a negotiation, an entrepreneur must set the agenda and desired goals. Entrepreneurs must also realize what arguments made by them will be more effective and how they should communicate with other parties. At the same time, the entrepreneur must also realize how powerful is the party on the other side of the table and how they can minimize conflict and maximize personal gain. As in any negotiation gaining trust of the party on the other side of the table is of utmost importance. Entrepreneurs can achieve this by enhancing rapport with the negotiating parties. Entrepreneurs can also enhance trust by lowering the impact of cultural differences between them and the negotiating parties. It is a known fact that people like and trust people who are like them and in negotiations it can lead to favorable outcomes.

There are numerous ways by which entrepreneurs can achieve favorable outcomes for themselves in negotiations. One such strategy is favor request, where the entrepreneur makes small favors for the other parties in negotiation. Such small favors generate return favors which might create value for the entrepreneur. Also, the entrepreneur can engage in adaptive behaviors where they alter their behaviors to match the behaviors of negotiating parties. Such adaptation can also have favorable outcomes for the entrepreneur.

Maximizing personal gain is the objective of every person engaging in negotiation. However, maximizing personal gain may not always be attainable. Based on the situation at hand and relative bargaining power of all parties in negotiation, the entrepreneur must decide to choose the integrative or distributive negotiation. It is not always beneficial to pursue the distributive negotiation when other parties in a negotiation have high bargaining power or there is a desire for long-term relationship with such parties.

There are strategies that entrepreneurs must avoid. Using deception and having a lack of empathy for other parties in negotiation can have a detrimental impact on the entrepreneurs. Trust is very important for negotiating with entrepreneurs and once broken it will be hard for entrepreneur to gain the lost credibility. Entrepreneurs must not drag negotiations by engaging in false negotiations and must ensure that they do not come across to other negotiating parties as information manipulators.

Key Terms

- Negotiation history
- Integrative vs distributive negotiation
- Trust
- Negotiation style
- Deception

Case

Austin grew up in a suburb of Chicago and always wanted to be an entrepreneur. At the age of 16, he started working as a freelance software coder and bought his first computer from the money he earned. He was not happy with the growth he had from the freelance work and decided to start a company. His company was initially making software solutions for other companies and had about five clients in the first year.

In the second year of his business venture, Austin had 10 clients and the orders he received from his clients gave him an insight into what his clients were selling to their clients. So instead of just selling software to clients, he decided to sell software and hardware solutions. He planned to build the software inhouse and source hardware from OEM manufacturers in China.

Very soon his dreams had a setback. He needed four major things for his idea to succeed. First, he needed capital from banks to be able to fund the operations. Second, he needed skilled software and hardware engineers who will be willing to work on his projects. Third, he needed market researchers who will evaluate market requirements and position custom products for different groups of consumers. Fourth, he needed suppliers in China who will supply him with the hardware at costs that are not detrimental to the profits.

Austin soon realized that he needed to build agenda and engage in negotiations with each of these four stakeholder groups. He approached the bank with a business plan and requested a loan of half a million dollars. The loan officer at the bank was not convinced that the business will be able to generate revenue to pay off the loan. Austin was requested to submit additional documentation related to his company's plans about taking products to market.

Austin's search for skilled hardware and software engineers did lead to surprises. The skilled engineers on the market were not sure about their career growth potential at his company and to work for a smaller company they wanted a much higher compensation as compared to their current established employers. Austin was perplexed and did not know how to negotiate with the engineers. Offering more money than his large competitors was not an option for him.

The market research agency he hired for doing preliminary market analysis provided him with some good news. Based on the report by the agency, there were only four competitors in the category he wanted to position his company. However, all four competitors were more than five years old and had established market share. To be able to successfully penetrate the market, Austin must offer discounts to consumers or come up with radical innovations that generate savings for consumers.

Austin also approached several Chinese hardware suppliers. To his surprise, the Chinese suppliers were already doing business with his competitors and did not seem willing to work with his company at the price he was offering them. They also had a minimum order quantity and Austin was not sure if he had the capital to purchase goods in bulk initially.

Austin for sure bit more than he could chew and wondered if he can make his venture succeed? However, such situations are an everyday issue for startup entrepreneurs. The best part is that such situations can sometimes be resolved by parties who use the right negotiation strategies.

Based on the chapter and the above-mentioned case, please answer the following questions:

Q.1 How should Austin negotiate with the bank? What strategies should he adopt to convince the loan officer?

Q.2 The engineers did want a higher compensation to work for a relatively younger company. How can Austin negotiate with the engineers such that he gets to use their expertise and does not have to pay more?

Q.3 The Chinese suppliers also do not wish to do business with him at the prices he offered. What deal can he negotiate with them to lower the acceptable prices and quantity?

References

Aydin. (2020). 'How 3 Guys Turned Renting Air Mattresses in Their Apartment into a $31 Billion Company, Airbnb'. 2021. https://www.businessinsider.com/how-airbnb -was-founded-a-visual-history-2016-2.

Batson, C. D., D. A. Lishner, A. Carpenter, L. Dulin, S. Harjusola-Webb, E. Stocks, et al. (2003). "…As You Would Have Them Do Unto You': Does Imagining Yourself in the Other's Place Stimulate Moral Action'. *Personality and Social Psychology Bulletin* 29, 1190–1201.

Batson, C. D., and N. Ahmad. (2001). 'Empathy-Induced Altruism in a Prisoner's Dilemma II: What If the Target of Empathy Has Defected?' *European Journal of Social Psychology* 31, 25–36.

Bennett, M. (1986). 'A Developmental Approach to Training for Intercultural Sensitivity'. *International Journal of Intercultural Relation* 10, 179–196.

Blanchard, S. J., K. A. Carlson, and J. D. Hyodo. (2016). 'The Favor Request Effect: Requesting a Favor From Consumers to Seal the Deal'. *Journal of Consumer Research* 42, 985–1001.

Bornstein, G., and O. Weisel. (2010). 'Punishment, Cooperation, and Cheater Detection in "Noisy" Social Exchange'. *Games* 1, 18–33.

Brewer, M. (1986). 'The Role of Ethnocentrism in Intergroup Conflict'. In W. G. Austin and S. Worchel (Eds.), *The Social Psychology of Intergroup Relations* (2nd ed., pp. 88–102). Monterey, CA: Brooks/Cole.

Britannica. (2021). 'List of Treaties'. 2021. https://www.britannica.com/topic/list-of -treaties-2030748.

Bronstein, I., N. Nelson, Z. Livnat, and R. Ben-Ari. (2012). 'Rapport in Negotiation: The Contribution of the Verbal Channel'. *The Journal of Conflict Resolution* 56(6), 1089–1115.

Burger, Jerry M. (1986). 'Increasing Compliance by Improving the Deal: The That's-Not-All Technique'. *Journal of Personality and Social Psychology* 51(2), 277–283.

Campbell, Margaret C., and Amna Kirmani (2000). 'Consumers' Use of Persuasion Knowledge: The Effects of Accessibility and Cognitive Capacity on Perceptions of an Influence Agent'. *Journal of Consumer Research* 27(1), 69–83.

Capes, M. (2013). *Communication or Conflict: Conferences: Their Nature, Dynamics, and Planning*. London: Routledge.

Carnevale, Peter J., and Edward J. Lawler (1986). 'Time Pressure and the Development of Integrative Agreements in Bilateral Negotiations'. *Journal of Conflict Resolution* 30, 636–659.

Chen, I., and Tseng, F. (2016). 'The Relevance of Communication Media in Conflict Contexts and Their Effectiveness: A Negotiation Experiment'. *Computed Human Behavior* 59, 134–141.

Darwin, C. (1913). *The origin of species by means of natural selection, or, the preservation of favoured races in the struggle for life*. Books, Incorporated, Publisher.

Davis, M. H. (1983b). 'Measuring Individual Differences in Empathy: Evidence for a Multidimensional Approach'. *Journal of Personality and Social Psychology* 44, 113–126.

De Dreu, C. K., L. R. Weingart, and S. Kwon. (2000). 'Influence of Social Motives on Integrative Negotiation: A Meta-Analytic Review and Test of Two Theories'. *Journal of Personality and Social Psychology* 78, 889–905.

Drolet, A. L., and M. W. Morris. 1995. 'Communication Media and Interpersonal Trust in Conflicts: The Role of Rapport and Synchrony of Nonverbal Behavior'. Paper Presented at the Academy of Management Meeting, Vancouver, Canada.

Dunbar, R. I. M. (1996). *Grooming, Gossip and the Evolution of Language*. London: Faber and Faber.

Emerson, Richard M. (1962). 'Power-Dependence Relations'. *American Sociological Review* 11, 31–40.

Gaspar, J. P., E. E. Levine, and M. E. Schweitzer. (2015). 'Why We Should Lie'. *Organizational Dynamics* 44, 306–309.

Gelfand, M. J., C. A. Fulmer, and L. E. Severance. (2011). 'The Psychology of Negotiation and Mediation'. In S. Zedeck (Ed.), *APA Handbook of Industrial and Organizational Psychology* (pp. 495–554). Washington, DC: American Psychological Association.

Glozman, E., Barak-Corren, N., and Yaniv, I. (2015). 'False negotiations: The art and science of not reaching an agreement'. *Journal of Conflict Resolution*, Vol. 59, No. 4, pp. 671–697.

Graham, J. L., D. K. Kim, C. Lin, and M. D. Robinson. (1988). 'Buyer-Seller Negotiations Around the Pacific Rim: Differences in Fundamental Exchange Processes'. *Journal of Consumer Research* 15, 48–54.

Graham, John L. (1986). 'The Problem-Solving Approach to Interorganizational Negotiations: A Laboratory Test'. *Journal of Business Research* 14, 271–286.

Grahe, J. E., and R. A. Sheman. (2007). 'An Ecological Examination of Rapport Using a Dyadic Puzzle Task'. *Journal of Social Psychology* 147, 453–475.

Kimmel, P. R. (1994). 'Cultural Perspectives on International Negotiations'. *Journal of Social Issues* 50, 179–196.

Koning, L., W. Steinel, I. Van Beest, and E. Van Dijk. (2011). 'Power and Deception in Ultimatum Bargaining'. *Organizational Behavior and Human Decision Processes* 115, 35–42.

Lewicki, R. J., and R. Hanke. (2012). 'Once Fooled, Shame on You! Twice Fooled, Shame on Me! What Deception Does to Deceivers and Victims: Implications for Negotiators When Ethicality is Unclear'. In B. M. Goldman and D. L. Shapiro (Eds.), *The*

Psychology of Negotiations in the 21st Century Workplace: New Challenges and New Solutions (pp. 211–244). New York, NY: Taylor and Francis.

Martin-Raugh, M. P., Kyllonen, P. C., Hao, J., Bacall, A., Becker, D., Kurzum, C., and Barnwell, P. (2020). 'Negotiation as an interpersonal skill: Generalizability of negotiation outcomes and tactics across contexts at the individual and collective levels'. *Computers in Human Behavior*, Vol. 104, p. 105966.

Maxwell, Sarah, Pete Nye, and Nicholas Maxwell. (2003). 'The Wrath of the Fairness-Primed Negotiator When the Reciprocity Norm is Violated'. *Journal of Business Research* 56(5), 399–409.

Miller, P. A., and N. Eisenberg. (1988). 'The Relation of Empathy to Aggressive and Externalizing/Antisocial Behavior'. *Psychological Bulletin* 103, 324–344.

Neale, M. A., and G. B. Northcraft. (1991). 'Behavioral Negotiation Theory: A Framework for Conceptualizing Dyadic Bargaining'. *Research in Organizational Behavior* 13, 147–190.

Pruitt, Dean G. (1983). 'Strategic Choice in Negotiation'. *American Behavioral Scientist* 27, 167–194.

Robinson, R. J., R. J. Lewicki, and E. M. Donahue. (2000). 'Extending and Testing a Five Factor Model of Ethical and Unethical Bargaining Tactics: Introducing the SINS Scale'. *Journal of Organizational Behavior* 21, 649–664.

Rubin, Jeffrey Z., and Bert R. Brown (1975). *The Social Psychology of Bargaining and Negotiation*. New York: Academic Press.

Sawyer, J., and Guetzkow, H. S. (1965). *Bargaining and Negotiation in International Relations*. City, ST: H. Rinehart and Winston, pp. 464–520.

Schweitzer, M. E., and Hsee, C. K. (2002). 'Stretching the truth: Elastic justification and motivated communication of uncertain information'. *Journal of Risk and Uncertainty*, Vol. 25, No. 2, pp. 185–201.

Schweitzer, M. E., L. A. DeChurch, and D. E. Gibson. (2005). 'Conflict Frames and the Use of Deception: Are Competitive Negotiators Less Ethical?' *Journal of Applied Social Psychology* 35, 2123–2149. DOI: 10.1111/j.1559-1816.2005.tb02212.x.

Thompson, L. L., J. Wang, and B. C. Gunia. (2010). 'Negotiation'. *Annual Review of Psychology* 61, 491–515.

Varey, R. J., T. Wood-harper, and B. Wood. (2002). 'A Theoretical Review of Management and Information Systems Using a Critical Communications Theory'. *Journal of Information Technology* 17, 229–239.

Walker, Orville, C., Jr. (1971). 'The Effects of Learning on Bargaining Behavior'. In Fred Allvine(Ed.), *Combined Proceedings: Spring and Eall Conferences*. Chicago: American Marketing Association, pp. 194–199.

Walton, Richard E., and Robert B. McKersie. (1965). *A Behavioral Theory of Labor Negotiations: An Analysis of Social Interaction Systems*. New York: McGraw-Hill.

Weitz, Barton A. (1978). 'The Relationship Between Salesperson Performance and Understanding of Customer Decision Making'. *Journal of Marketing Research* 15, 501–516.

Yan, D., and J. Pena-Marin. (2017). 'Round Off the Bargaining: The Effects of Offer Roundness on Willingness to Accept'. *Journal of Consumer Research* 44, 381–395.

Young, M. J., C. W. Bauman, N. Chen, and A. Bastardi. (2012). 'The Pursuit of Missing Information in Negotiation'. *Organizational Behavior and Human Decision Processes* 117(1), 88–95. DOI: 10.1016/j.obhdp.2011.09.004.

PART III

STRATEGY, PLANNING AND TACTICS IN NEGOTIATION

Chapter 6

NEGOTIATION ESSENTIALS: WHAT ALL A STARTUP ENTREPRENEUR CANNOT AFFORD TO MISS?

Learning Objectives

1. Understand the role of planning and scripting in negotiation
2. Exploring priorities of negotiating parties and utilizing winning strategies
3. Review concepts of BATNA and ZOPA
4. Importance of offering alternatives and de-anchoring negotiations
5. Tactical challenges and neutralization of dirty tricks

Opening Scenario: **Simon & Schuster vs Barnes and Noble**

When months of negotiation with publishing house Simon & Schuster reached a standoff, Barnes and Noble attempted to gain leverage by significantly reducing its orders of Simon & Schuster titles and engaging in other hardball negotiation tactics, such as refusing to book the publisher's authors for in-store readings. Given that Barnes and Noble sells about 20 percent of consumer books in the United States, Simon & Schuster editors and their associated agents and writers were "apoplectic" about the bookseller's decision to use them as a bargaining chip.

As the last major retail bookstore chain in the United States, Barnes and Noble has been pressing publishers to make steep concessions to enable its survival against Amazon.com and other online retailers. The bookstore chain reportedly sought significantly lower wholesale prices for Simon & Schuster's books and tried to charge the publisher more to display its title in its stores. Simon & Schuster said it simply could not afford to abide by Barnes and Noble's terms.

The two companies later issued a joint statement saying they had resolved their disagreement and looked forward to jointly promote Simon & Schuster's books. Though details of the agreement remain unknown, any gains they achieved would be undercut by the profits each side lost during the months of impasse, when Simon & Schuster books were missing from display tables and shelves. Such penalties often end up undercutting both parties to a negotiation.

Planning and Scripting in Negotiation

Planning is an essential strategic entrepreneurial activity. In the case of negotiations involving entrepreneurs with other entrepreneurs and organizations, planning is even more critical. The reason for the claim is that entrepreneurs oversee their own decisions and do not have the brainpower afforded to large corporations. Large corporations can form committees to oversee negotiation planning and have set a standard of procedures for negotiations. For entrepreneurs, the activity is one man's job.

When entrepreneurs negotiate with organizations, the organizations usually have relatively higher bargaining power than the entrepreneur. Research suggests that parties in negotiation with high bargaining power can achieve better outcomes for themselves than parties with relatively low bargaining power (Dwyer & Walker, 1981). To avoid such situations the entrepreneur must create agendas before entering a negotiation. An agenda is like a script that details potential structured discussions between negotiating parties as well as issues to be discussed (Pruitt, 1981). The entrepreneur might also face time constraints in negotiations if negotiations are about issues that are time critical such as perishable goods and expiring contracts. Such instances put an additional burden on the entrepreneur leading to less favorable outcomes if proper agendas are not utilized.

We know that time constraints increase acceptance of less favorable outcome by a party with lower bargaining power (Walton & McKersie, 1965). One such example is the ban on import of pineapples grown in Taiwan by Chinese authorities in March 2021. In this case, pineapple growers in Taiwan utilized the help of Taiwanese government officials to negotiate with Chinese government and simultaneously negotiate alternate markets for their produce. The unexpected ban on the export of pineapple produce put immense time constraints on Taiwanese pineapple growers and a favorable outcome would not have been possible without a carefully crafted agenda.

Exploring Priorities of Parties in Negotiation

Before entering formal negotiations, it is essential to understand the priorities of all negotiating parties on the other side of the table. The best way to explore the priorities of other negotiating parties is to view the world through their eyes. Perspective-taking is an important concept for entrepreneurial negotiators. Entering negotiations with a purely self-serving agenda and ignoring priorities of other parties will reduce the chance of other parties reaching an agreement. Perspective-taking is a thought process that involves imagining yourself in someone else's shoes.

In any negotiation two or more parties are strategically involved in getting the best outcome for everyone which might not be possible by voluntarily accepting the first round of offers from other parties (Lewicki & Stark, 1996: 71). As the first round of offers might not be accepted right away by other negotiating parties, passing the first round of offers with perspective-taking and keeping priorities of other parties in mind can help improve the future direction of negotiations. We know that perspective-takers who utilize information about other parties in a negotiation enjoy positive relationships and are more likely to be recipients of concessions (Gehlbach et al., 2015). The concession for negotiating entrepreneurs can be in the form of acceptance of offers that might not have been accepted under different circumstances. Positive relationships with other negotiating parties also help entrepreneurs as they have relatively lower bargaining power unless negotiating with similar entrepreneurs.

Passing offers based on perspective-taking also leads to lasting agreements between the entrepreneur and other parties in negotiation. The reason for the claim is due to the impact of information exchange. We know that trading information about needs and interests helps negotiators achieve outcomes that serve the needs of all parties, and such outcomes last longer as compared to ones achieved without information exchange (Pruitt, 1981). Not only does information exchange helps achieve lasting agreements, but it also speeds up the process of negotiations in general. When negotiating parties are aware of the needs and priorities of other parties, they can adjust their offers early in the negotiation leading to a faster conclusion of negotiation process.

Winning Negotiation Strategies for Entrepreneurs

Utilizing positive emotions: Entrepreneurs can potentially utilize positive emotions to alter the outcomes of negotiations. Emotions have a unique property that they are contagious among people. When entrepreneurs are in negotiations, they can exhibit positive emotions that will be transferred to other parties. The interesting thing about positive emotions is that people experiencing them tend to view other people more favorably (Bower, 1991). This phenomenon can do wonders for entrepreneur as it helps build favorability and trust for entrepreneurs among other negotiating parties.

Representativeness: The principle of representativeness relies on the tendency that people tend to generalize about a person or object based on relatively few attributes. The concept was introduced in 1971 by Tversky and Kahneman and is highly relevant in scenarios where entrepreneurs enter in negotiations with other parties. Considering the relatively small size of entrepreneur's business and the lack of trust in the entrepreneurs' abilities and character, it is in the best interest of the entrepreneur to showcase the most positive qualities of their business or personality. Merely bragging about personality and business might do more harm than good. The optimal strategy in this case is to focus on verifiable past achievements rather than highlighting vague and boastful positive attributes.

Say what they want to hear: It is essential for an entrepreneur to make sure they shape their communication that best suits the mind-set of people they are communicating with. People vary in terms of their propensity to incline toward growth or fixed mind-set. The two mind-sets were introduced by Dweck (1996). People with fixed mind-set are the ones who wish to maintain favorable personal reputation and competence; whereas, people with growth mind-set tend to favor situations that help them make improvements to their personal self or surroundings.

In situations where the entrepreneurs do not have high bargaining power or are dealing with difficult negotiators, it is best to understand the mind-set of the other parties and shape the communication in ways that best aligns with other parties' mind-sets.

BATNA, ZOPA and Value Creation

BATNA stands for "best alternative to negotiated agreement." In any negotiation, parties have an alternate option that can be chosen as a solution instead of entering negotiations with other parties. This alternate option acts as a reference point to evaluate whether negotiations will bring them a better alternative as compared to the existing option. BATNA is the term used to describe the reference point for parties when they enter negotiations (Thompson et al., 2010).

For example, an entrepreneur sources raw materials from a present supplier but wishes to get a better deal for his purchase in the future. The incentive to find a new supplier is to enhance personal bargaining power and lower costs. To lower the costs of raw materials and maximize profits, the entrepreneur contacts multiple suppliers of raw materials in the market. The entrepreneur gets lucky and receives interest from three suppliers who can potentially supply the required quality and quantity of the raw material. But the suppliers do not wish to disclose the price they can offer before negotiations about quality and quantity. The entrepreneur sets up a meeting with all three suppliers and the first supplier offers a price slightly lower than the existing supplier. The price offered by the new supplier becomes a new BATNA for the entrepreneur as it is the lowest price offered to him so far.

In future, the entrepreneur also receives price offers from the other two suppliers after extensive negotiations about needs and priorities. One of these suppliers offers a price slightly higher than his BATNA but the quality offered by this supplier is exactly what the entrepreneur needs. The entrepreneur is tempted to enter further negotiations, and it is the BATNA that offers him an edge in negotiations. To get a favorable personal outcome, the entrepreneur informs the supplier that another supplier has already offered a price lower than the price being offered by the supplier. In the end, the entrepreneur strikes a deal with the negotiating supplier at the lowest price with the highest desired quality of raw material that nobody else offered so far.

Thus, we can witness how negotiators can potentially use BATNA for their benefit and get the most favorable outcome. The strategy is relatively more important for entrepreneurs because of relative lack of capital and the need to secure lowest prices for their raw materials. BATNA is also important when entrepreneurs make offers to potential customers as they can quote prices they are already getting for their products and services. Providing a reference point to potential customers might potentially change the outcome of negotiations in favor of the entrepreneur.

When two or more parties enter a negotiation, it is very important for each one of them to evaluate the needs and priorities of each party. If they do not take into account the needs and priorities of other parties, there is a chance that all parties may build agendas that are outside the zone of possible agreement (ZOPA). ZOPA is the range of possible negotiation on different issues and defines whether the negotiating parties will ever reach an agreement on these issues. If negotiating parties come up with offers that lay outside ZOPA, there is a chance that the negotiations may not even initiate. In unlikely circumstances that they do initiate, it is possible that such negotiations may never reach an agreement. Thus, it is very important for negotiating parties to ensure that their agenda includes offers that lie within ZOPA of other parties or it will be waste of time and resources for all parties.

ZOPA and BATNA allow negotiators to create value for each other. Value is created when all parties in a negotiation understand and address the needs and priorities of other parties and incorporate actions that satisfy the identified needs. Some opportunistic parties in negotiations might claim that they created value by addressing their needs at the expense of other parties. Such instances do not account for value creation.

Value creation is a process and is contingent on healthy relationship management between negotiating parties (Olekalns & Brett, 2008). Healthy relationships cannot be maintained if some parties are solely looking forward to only maximize value for themselves. For entrepreneurs, it is essential to incorporate value creation in their negotiation strategies. If entrepreneurs engage in tactics that only generate value for themselves, there is a good chance that the relationship with other parties will be soured.

De-anchoring in Negotiation

An example of poor ZOPA evaluation and incorporation by a negotiating party is to engage in the cognitive bias of anchoring. Sometimes negotiating parties only wish to create value for themselves or have a poor understanding of the needs and priorities of other parties. In such cases, they engage in anchoring by paying too much emphasis on their offer which might be out of ZOPA for other parties. Such behavior can have a catastrophic outcome for negotiations unless other parties de-anchor the party engaging in such behaviors. Other parties also have the option of providing a counteroffer which is in their ZOPA but such behaviors may not resolve the anchoring bias. Before providing a realistic offer within their ZOPA, other parties in negotiation must make sure to de-anchor by providing a realistic and just explanation of why the offer is not credible and does not serve their interest. Such explanations will help the negotiations move forward and potentially create value for all parties.

Multiple Alternatives and Deadlocks

A deadlock is an undesirable condition in any negotiation. Deadlocks occur when parties in negotiations feel that their substantive, procedural or emotional interests are unmet Sycara (1991). There are numerous ways to resolve a deadlock and an effective way is by offering multiple alternatives. Offering multiple alternatives works in many ways. First, it makes unsatisfied parties in negotiation believe that other parties are addressing procedural issues by incorporating additional effort to come up with multiple alternatives. Second, offering multiple alternatives allows unsatisfied parties to get a sense of perceived joint concerns from other parties. Third, multiple alternatives help unsatisfied parties get a sense that other parties are ready to make changes to past decisions and are ready to come up with more solutions to satisfy the unmet needs. Resolving deadlocks must be a top priority for entrepreneurs as deadlocks can lead to termination of negotiations if the unsatisfied party's needs are not addressed. Entrepreneurs can incorporate the strategy of offering multiple alternatives to make sure they potentially generate value for all parties in negotiations.

Tactical Challenges

Most negotiations involve tactical behaviors by some parties who are opportunistic. Tactics involve behaviors that may or may not be perceived as ethical based on the type and context of negotiation. Tactics involve behaviors such as deception, misrepresentation of data and projecting personal preferences that might not be a true representation of ideal preferences (Anton, 1990). Some negotiators engage in misrepresenting their needs and preferences to mislead other parties. Such behaviors may not constitute outright lying but essentially constitute as tactics. So, the key question to be answered is what tactics are acceptable and can be used by negotiators without being unethical. Under any circumstance, outright lying is not an acceptable form of tactic (O'Connor & Carnevale, 1997). However, when entrepreneurs negotiate, they can utilize passive forms of dishonesty such as lies of omission. When entrepreneurs negotiate, they are not obliged to reveal all personal information and can hide information that might be used against them. Such tactics help entrepreneurs negotiate better as it lowers the chances of other parties making negative judgments about the entrepreneur.

It can be useful for entrepreneurs to not disclose information about past suppliers of raw materials, ownership in other businesses or personal preferences such as quality. For example, there are instances when entrepreneurs negotiate with suppliers and the suppliers disclose technical details about the quality of materials themselves. It makes no sense for the entrepreneur to disclose their preferences about quality. If suppliers know the quality preferences of the entrepreneur, they might modify their agenda to increase the offer price as their products meet quality requirements of the entrepreneur.

Dirty Tricks in Negotiation

There is a thin line between ethical tactics and unethical tactical behaviors in negotiations. Deception is a problem in negotiation, and it is critical for entrepreneurs to detect and neutralize deceptive tactics. Negotiators use deception because they do not want other parties to know the truth. The reason people deceive is that revelation of truth might hamper chances of their goal attainment (Levine, 2014). The goal is usually self-serving and generates personal value with total disregard to value generation for other parties.

A common dirty trick in negotiation is when parties finalize the deal, but other parties never actually complete the deal. The party with intentions to complete the deal feels that the deal is complete and drops the other. The parties playing this trick want to generate desperation and uncertainty among other parties. Knowing that other parties are desperate to close the deal, the party playing the trick offers a revised deal which increases the benefits to the party playing the trick. In such cases, it is best to drop the deal as there is a good chance that the party playing the trick may not stick to the terms of revised deal even in future.

Some negotiators also play the trick of never revealing the key decision makers on their end. Trick includes finalizing the deal by promising other parties that conditions are acceptable. However, a few days or weeks later, other parties are informed that the key decision maker who was not introduced earlier is not happy with the deal. Other parties are also served with a revised deal based on inputs from the mysterious key decision maker. To avoid such situation, it is best to talk to key decision maker from the beginning and not waste time negotiating with people who do not hold decision making authority.

Some negotiators also play the trick of information overload by burdening other parties with excessive amounts of information that may or may not be relevant. In such cases, it is advisable to ignore such information and request parties playing such tricks to only show precise and relevant information relevant to negotiation.

Chapter Summary

Startup entrepreneurs often have limited capital and compromised bargaining power but at the same time to expand their business they must engage in an extensive number of negotiations. Such negotiations can be with suppliers of raw materials, potential employees, lenders or potential customers. It is essential for entrepreneurs to equip themselves with the essentials of negotiations which will help them achieve favorable outcomes for themselves.

Entering a formal negotiation with other parties without an agenda can be disastrous. The entrepreneurs must do research on what their priorities and needs are, as well as what are the perceived needs of other parties in the negotiation. In presence of a written agenda, the entrepreneur can review and discuss all issues that need to be negotiated. When the negotiation begins, the entrepreneur can utilize multiple strategies outlined in the chapter which can help the entrepreneur achieve a favorable outcome for themselves.

BATNA and ZOPA are two key concepts that are relevant in this scenario. The entrepreneurs can utilize BATNA as a tool for convincing other parties faster. As BATNA acts as a reference point in negotiations, it helps people make faster decisions. ZOPA offers all parties in negotiation a potential range of agreeability. Any party negotiating outside ZOPA might attract backlash from other negotiating parties.

The chapter also outlines the concept of de-anchoring. Some negotiating parties utilize the strategy of anchoring, and they may not do it intentionally. Anchoring is a result of information asymmetry between parties and poor evaluation of ZOPA. De-anchoring is a great strategy to move negotiations forward by avoiding deadlocks. Along with de-anchoring, entrepreneurs can utilize the strategy of offering multiple alternatives to avoid deadlocks. Finally, it is important to understand the tactics used by negotiators and how entrepreneurs can identify such tactics and neutralize any potential impact of unethical tactics.

Key Terms

- Negotiation planning
- Winning strategies
- BATNA, ZOPA
- De-anchoring
- Deadlocks
- Tactics and tricks

Review Questions

Q. 1 Discuss the importance of setting agendas in negotiations. Outline how it is important for startup entrepreneurs.

Q. 2 Why is exploring the priorities of other parties in negotiation essential? Identify the drawbacks of not identifying such priorities.

Q. 3 What are BATNA and ZOPA? Why are they of importance to startup entrepreneurs?

Q. 4 Does offering multiple alternatives help in negotiations?

Q. 5 How can negotiators identify and neutralize dirty tricks in negotiation?

Case

Mumbi is a college senior at a university in Port Au-Prince, Haiti. Mumbi is a social work major and aspires to help the people of her country. While browsing the internet, Mumbi came across an article that emphasized that Haiti has the highest levels of child malnutrition in the world. She was moved by the article and decided to start a business that will help reduce child malnutrition in Haiti.

To accomplish her goal, Mumbi decided to start a staple food distribution mobile application where parents of malnourished children can get direct support from donors. Donors can donate food to families by buying the food at the nearest grocery stores. The families can then pick up the food at their convenience. To build the mobile application, Mumbi must raise money for developing the application. She contacted multiple application developers and informed them about her idea. The application developers had a meeting with her, but she made a big mistake. She was not prepared for the meeting and did not know what all features her app should have. After one month she met the developers again, and they agreed to build her app for free after carefully considering the humanitarian impact of the project.

Local grocery stores played a major role in the success of her project. Mumbi contacted multiple local grocery stores but soon realized it was impossible to reach out individually to each grocery store. Owner of every grocery store also had their own demands and restrictions on how they wanted to do business with Mumbi's application. To solve the problem, she contacted the grocery store owner association and negotiated terms and conditions of working with the application. This time she was prepared and utilized data collected from contacting individual store owners to craft her agenda and offers. The data helped Mumbi to generate creative and constructive feedback for unrealistic demands from the association.

Finally, Mumbi rolled out her application. However, she ran into big problems. Numerous families collected food donated even when they did not have malnourished children. To solve the problem, she hired a few volunteers who would interview each family one by one. The strategy failed as it was impossible to interview each family and evaluate the truth of their claims. She devised a creative solution. Mumbi formed virtual communities on her application where people within a region would certify the presence of malnourished children in other people's households. The solution worked and Mumbi felt great she gave back to her community.

Based on the chapter and the above-mentioned case, answer the following questions:

Q. 1 What wrong did Mumbi do when she met the application developers and how did she fix it?

Q. 2 How did Mumbi utilize ZOPA with grocery store owners?

Q. 3 Did Mumbi utilize de-anchoring in her strategies over time? How?

Q. 4 How did she neutralize dirty tricks used by families who falsely claimed benefits?

References

Anton, R. J. (1990). Drawing the line: An exploratory test of ethical behavior in negotiation. *The International Journal of Conflict Management*, *1*, 265–280. DOI: 10.1108/eb022683.

Bower, G. H. (1991). Mood congruity of social judgments. In J. P. Forgas (Ed.), *Emotion and Social Judgments* (pp. 31–53). Sydney: Pergamon Press.

Dweck, C. S. (1996). Implicit theories as organizers of goals and behavior. In *The Psychology of Action: Linking Cognition and Motivation to Behavior*. New York: Guilford.

Dwyer, F. R., & Walker, O. C. (1981). Bargaining in an asymmetrical power structure. *Journal of Marketing, 45*, 104–115.

Gehlbach, Hunter, Marietta, Geoff, King, Aaron M., Karutz Cody, Bailenson, Jeremy N., & Dede, Chris. (2015). Many ways to walk a mile in another's moccasins. *Computers in Human Behavior, 52*, 523–532.

Levine, E. E., & Schweitzer, M. E. (2014). Are liars ethical? On the tension between benevolence and honesty. *Journal of Experimental Social Psychology, 53*, 107–117.

Lewicki, R. J.. & Stark, N. (1996). What is ethically appropriate in negotiations: An empirical examination of bargaining tactics. *Social Justice Research, 9*, 69–95. DOI: 10.1007/BF02197657.

O'Connor, K. M., & Carnevale, P. (1997). A nasty but effective negotiation strategy: Misrepresentation of a common-value issue. *Personality and Social Psychology Bulletin, 23*, 504–515. DOI: 10.1177/0146167297235006.

Olekalns, M., & Brett, J. M. (2008). Beyond the deal: Next generation negotiation skills. *Negotiation and Conflict Management Research, 1*, 309–314.

Pruitt, Dean G. (1981). *Negotiation Behavior*. New York: Academic Press.

Sycara, K. P. (1991). 'Problem restructuring in negotiation'. *Management Science*, Vol. 37, No. 10, pp. 1248–1268.

Thompson, Leigh L., Wang, Jiunwen, & Gunia, Brian C. (2010). Negotiation. *Annual Review of Psychology, 61*, 491–515.

Tversky, A., & Kahneman, D. (1971). Belief in the law of small numbers. *Psychological Bulletin, 76*(2), 105–110. DOI: 10.1037/h0031322.

Walton, R. E., & McKersie, R. B. (1965). *A Behavioral Theory of Labor Negotiations*. New York and London: McGraw-Hill.

Chapter 7

TEN LAWS OF NEGOTIATION
FOR ENTREPRENEURS

Learning Objectives

1. To understand the importance of distinction between a meeting and a negotiation meeting
2. What are disastrous outcomes and how to manage them
3. To understand the art of probing in negotiation
4. Evaluate the importance of timing in making offers
5. Overview concepts of empathy, trust and irrationality. Study their importance in the context of negotiation

Opening Profile: Starbucks and Kraft Foods

Back in 2013, a three-year negotiation and dispute between Starbucks and Kraft Foods over the distribution of Starbucks packaged coffee in grocery stores was finally resolved. On November 12, 2013, an arbitrator determined that Starbucks had breached its agreement with Kraft and ordered the coffeemaker to pay the food giant $ 2.75 billion.

After negotiating an agreement in 1998, Kraft began selling Starbucks packaged coffee through grocery stores. In 2010, with sales of its packaged coffee reaching about $ 500 million annually, Starbucks offered to buy Kraft out of the contract for $ 750 million. Starbucks wanted greater flexibility to sell the single-serve coffee pods that were hot at the time. The company's agreement with Kraft limited Starbucks to selling pods that worked only in Kraft's Tassimo machines.

Kraft objected to the deal termination, but Starbucks broke off the business relationship, nonetheless. Since then, Starbucks' share of single-serve pod market and grocery-store products has grown significantly. The parties' dispute over Starbucks' termination of their partnership moved to arbitration when the two sides were unable to settle it on their own.

The business dispute illustrates how the fluid nature of marketplace trends can cause negotiated business agreements to become undesirable over time. In their original agreement, Kraft and Starbucks would have been wise to agree upon set times for renegotiation, during which they would have had leeway to revisit existing deal terms in the face of changed economic and industry conditions. They could also have negotiated conditions for ending the agreement early, such as cancellation penalties and other forms of compensation.

Sometimes you and your counterpart can draft the agreement on your own. Larger agreements and dispute settlements, on the other hand, typically have legal provisions drafted by a lawyer or a third party. Unfortunately, the handoff from dealmakers to deal drafters is error-prone, and these errors can have real business consequences.

Law 1: Call a Negotiation Meeting, Not Just a Meeting

Negotiation is a social activity that involves multiple parties getting strategically involved to reach a decision on a particular topic of interest. The topic of interest can vary based on the nature and setting of negotiation and can include resolution of conflict between parties, discussions of future partnership possibilities, and so on. The primary reason for the existence of negotiations is the fact that the parties involved in negotiations can conclude without engaging in extensive discussions about possible outcomes. We know that negotiations are essential as parties in negotiation are not willing to accept the first round of offers from other parties (Lewicki & Stark, 1996, p. 71).

Pursuant to intuition, the first thought that comes to people's mind about negotiation is a meeting. But in fact, the purpose and process of negotiation are different from a simple meeting. Meetings in general can be classified based on their purpose. A casual meeting without a purpose in a business setting is purely exploratory in nature and serves the purpose of building bonds among businesspeople and opening doors for future collaboration. On the other hand, meetings with a purpose are conducted between businesspeople who have partnered in past and have an issue, concern or objective to be accomplished. In such circumstances, it is essential to note that meetings classified as negotiations have one thing in common. All parties want to reach a mutually acceptable outcome that is equitable and satisfies the needs of all. Thus, negotiation meetings offer businesspeople capabilities to resolve issues and foster equitable growth by communicating their perspectives, needs and concerns. When preparing for a negotiation meeting it is essential for negotiators to create an agenda. An agenda is primarily information about the issues to be brought to the table and structures of discussion through which the issues will be addressed by individuals and groups (Pruitt, 1981). Negotiators must also ensure that they understand the perspective of other parties in negotiation and do not strive to maximize their personal gains solely. A meeting without an agenda, timeline or perspective-taking might not be successful as it lacks purpose and structure.

Law 2: Applaud the Valid Arguments of the Other Party

No negotiation is complete without the presentation of arguments from different parties in negotiation. The issues and arguments that are discussed in negotiation are usually outlined in the agendas of all parties in negotiation. Sometimes the negotiating parties share their agendas with other parties to let them prepare for arguments and rebuttals. The arguments might vary in terms of their validity. Some negotiating parties might have arguments that are not reasonable and maximize solely their personal gains. On the other hand, reasonable and just arguments are also brought up in the agenda, and they are perceived as valid if they are based on facts and do not solely serve the interests of the party bringing up the argument.

Parties in negotiation are essentially composed of people and when they bring a valid or invalid argument to the table, it elicits responses from other parties. It is essential for other parties in negotiation to applaud valid arguments brought to the table. The reason for such a claim is based on the concept of personality. Agreeing or disagreeing with a valid argument will lead parties in negotiation to form judgments about the personality of people they are negotiating with. Personality has five distinct traits which are conscientiousness, agreeableness, extraversion, emotional stability and openness (Digman, 1990). People perceived as conscientious are predisposed to be disciplined, dependable and disciplined and are more likely to be preferred in hiring for jobs (Dunn et al., 1995). People perceived as agreeable are predisposed to be tolerant, cooperative and selfless (Digman, 1990). People who applaud the valid arguments of other parties in negotiation are more likely to be perceived as conscientious and agreeable. Perceptions of these traits can do wonders for negotiators as applause of valid arguments is an expressed behavior. We know that expressed behaviors of negotiating parties can foster trust (Grahe & Sheman, 2007). Enjoying the trust of other parties in negotiation can do wonders as it may facilitate faster the equitable outcome of negotiations.

Law 3: Keep Ready Your Plan of Action Against a Tragic End

The purpose of a negotiation is to strategically discuss the potential outcome of a problem or opportunity wherein the arguments of all parties are considered to reach the outcome. In some cases, certain parties in negotiation enter the discussion with some assumptions regarding the outcome of negotiations. The assumptions can be about the process or outcome of the negotiations. Holding assumptions that the outcome of negotiation will be exactly as perceived before negotiations can lead to disappointment. No party in negotiation desires a less than favorable outcome for themselves. However, sometimes circumstances change quickly due to the dynamics in negotiations, and it is likely that some parties face a terrible outcome for themselves. Holding the assumption that disastrous outcomes will happen to other people instead of personal disastrous outcomes is a psychological phenomenon. The phenomenon is termed as the third-person effect. Based on third-person effect, people are more likely to evaluate possibility of disastrous outcomes for other people instead of themselves, and such thoughts are based on personal biases people hold (Davison, 1983). Thus, it is essential for all parties in negotiations to be prepared for any kind of outcomes including disastrous outcomes for themselves as well as for other parties.

Preparing for disastrous outcomes of negotiations is not an easy task. First, parties in negotiation enter the discussion in good faith and want favorable outcomes for themselves. Second, as the disastrous outcomes are not expected, they lead to high levels of ambivalence and frustration. It is not possible for parties in negotiations to have action plans ready for a disastrous outcome before the initiation of discussions. The reason for claim is that outcomes of negotiations unfold as the discussions in negotiations progress. However, in later stages of negotiations, the possibility and characteristics of disastrous outcomes can be relatively overtly visible to different parties. To overcome the negative impact of such disastrous outcomes, concrete actions must be taken. Such actions are based on potential desirable outcomes of actions and on potential feasibility of the outcomes. The theory of reasoned action posits that people engage in certain actions if they have viewed favorable outcome for themselves by undertaking actions and such actions are feasible (Fishbein & Ajzen, 1977). Thus, as discussions in negotiations unfold, it is critical for parties to understand the potential outcomes and if disastrous outcomes are sensed then they must be remedied in real time by formulating corrective actions based on desirability and feasibility.

Law 4: Ending Well Is Indispensable; Focus on Means Is Inevitable Too!

Negotiations are set up to achieve an equitable solution to a problem or opportunity and should conclude with a solution that maximizes gains for specific parties. The role of outcomes is critical to negotiations, but the outcomes cannot be achieved without the right process to achieve such outcomes. If the process is flawed, the possibility of achieving means is slim to none. The process of negotiations includes ensuring that there is an adequate rapport between parties, linguistic and communication barriers are addressed, key information such as agenda is shared between parties, inter- and intra-group tensions are resolved by mediation, time constraints are communicated, information privacy concerns among parties are upheld and dirty tricks in negotiation are taken care of.

Let us assume that an entrepreneur named Frank travels to China to source products to sell on Amazon. Frank did his market research and found out that the consumers are leaving bad reviews for an electric can opener sold by a leading brand. Consumers complain that the can opener is too noisy, overpriced and sometimes malfunction. The leading brand has not resolved the issue and continues to sell the faulty product. Frank finds out that a Chinese manufacturer is selling a similar can opener in China with none of the reported issues. Frank books the first flight to China and contacts the manufacturer. The manufacturer decides to hold a negotiation meeting to discuss the terms and conditions of their partnership. Frank submits his agenda before meeting and discloses why the product will sell well in the United States and how many he can sell in the next 24 months. According to his beliefs, Frank thought that disclosing such information will get him a better outcome in negotiation and he will secure a good price as well as an exclusivity contract. However, the Chinese manufacturer decided to share only a limited agenda and in negotiation, the manufacturer revealed that their product is the right fit for an unmet need in the United States. They stipulated a condition that for Frank to sell the product in the United States, the product must be labeled with the manufacturer's brand. If Frank wants to sell the product under his private brand, then the manufacturer will charge a 20 percent premium on price and the contract will be valid for only one year. At the expiration of contract, the manufacturer will sell the product directly under their brand name or to other brands in the United States. Frank was devastated by the outcome of negotiation and realized he made fatal mistakes in negotiation process by revealing too much private information. The damage was done for Frank, and he decided to take the first flight back home and look for another product to sell on Amazon.

Law 5: Probing Is an Art in Negotiation: Learn It!

A famous and thought-provoking quote by Heraclitus (c.535 BC–475 BC): "If you do not expect the unexpected, you will not find it; for it is hard to be sought out, and difficult," makes us wonder about the importance of expectancies in life. Human beings engage in deep thoughts and probe the future based on personal experiences, experiences from past events and relationships with other people. In most cases, people tend to shape a rosy outlook for themselves in future wherein their expectations will come true, and things will go as planned. However, things do not often go as planned and setbacks happen. The same is true for negotiation meetings as expectations may not come true leading to less than desired outcomes. Thus, it is essential for negotiators to think about all possible outcomes of a negotiation and do not rely on the best-case or worst-case scenario. Negotiators should engage in perspective-taking and view the world wearing shoes of other parties in negotiation. This will help negotiators achieve a much broader outlook on the situation and make unbiased informed inferences.

Some negotiators also engage in the practice of bottom-line mentality which can be disastrous to the outcome of negotiations. When people engage in bottom-line mentality, their behavior is perceived as myopic by others as bottom-line mentality is associated with neglect of others' considerations, being unethical while focusing on maximizing personal gain (Greenbaum et al., 2012). There is nothing wrong with emphasis on elevating personal gain, but it should not be the sole emphasis and at the expense of overlooking other people's interests. In negotiation settings, it is essential for parties to probe the needs of all parties and make sure that shape their agenda and discussion in a way that addresses other parties' interests. Failure to understand and probe other parties' interests will most likely lead to early termination of negotiation with no concrete outcome.

Law 6: Making Offers Is Good: The Question of Timing Matters!

Negotiations involve parties making offers after due consideration of agenda and arguments brought up in discussions. Some parties tend to rely on heuristics avoiding engagement in cognitive processing of other parties' agenda and pass offers prematurely. Offers delivered prematurely can lead to reactance among members and other parties. The reactance varies in valence and can be positive or negative. There might be situations where offers delivered prematurely generate positive valenced emotions among members of other parties. Such instances occur when the offer undermines the interests of the party passing the offer and the interests of other parties meet or exceed their expectations. Such scenarios are rare and most often prematurely passed offers predominantly serve the interests of parties passing the offer. Instances like these are detrimental to success of negotiations as other parties might presume that party passing premature offers are trying to assert dominance and are not interested in negotiating. For negotiations to achieve a win-win outcome it is essential to withhold offers to the point where all parties have presented their arguments, interests and demands.

It is also essential to understand what the nature of offer is and how it is communicated. According to the construal level theory proposed by Trope and Liberman (2010), messages are more persuasive when message features are congruent with the construal levels of parties receiving the messages (Rim et al., 2015). Messages can vary in terms of concreteness or abstractness. Concrete messages rely on secondary attributes such as exact financial return from entering a partnership. On the other hand, abstract messages rely on primary attributes such as enhanced brand value created by partnerships between parties. People also perceive an event to happen in near or distant future which in turn shapes their construal. Events that are believed to happen in distant future are classified as abstract construal thoughts whereas events happening in near future are classified as concrete construal thoughts. A persuasive message relying on concrete information such as immediate financial gain is more effective when such an event will happen in near future. For events likely to take place in distant future, messages relying on abstract persuasive information such as enhanced brand value are more effective. Parties in negotiation can shape their persuasive message content to enhance its effectiveness based on the fact whether the event related to event will happen in near or distant future.

Law 7: Avoid Taking Up Multiple Interests in One Go

Parties craft their agendas to formally address their interests and needs. However, some parties engage in the practice of overindulging in maximizing the breadth and depth of their interests and needs. Such instances are not ideal due to three reasons. First, negotiations are time bound and it is best to stick to discussing core issues and come to a mutually beneficial resolution. Parties who maximize the number of issues in their agendas risk early termination of negotiations as other parties may not have temporal, cognitive resources to discuss all the issues. Second, parties who include too many issues in their agenda risk being branded as greedy. Even though all the issues may be legitimate, too many issues might be perceived as an act of opportunism or greed. Third, inclusion of too many issues might lead to inconclusive negotiations as parties are likely to split their cognitive capabilities among variety of tasks leading to exhaustion.

When parties bring too many issues to table and negotiations are not terminated early, excessive issues are likely to have depletory psychological impact on parties. The concept of split attention is applicable in this scenario. When people process multiple pieces of information, it overburdens their working memory leading to split attention (Kalyuga et al., 1999). Split attention is positively related to excessive cognitive load among people processing different pieces of information (Sweller et al., 1998). Such situations are not desirable as cognitive overload leads to some information to be ignored by people suffering from the overload (Mayer et al., 2001). Parties bringing up too many issues might feel that bringing many issues to the table will make others feel that they did their job well. However, such practices usually have deleterious effects on outcome of negotiations and are best avoided.

Law 8: Empathy Can Cultivate Mutual Interests—Cultivate It!

During these negotiation meetings, people disclose their thoughts and emotions. Other people may or may not show empathy toward the expressed thoughts and feelings based on their personalities. Empathy is the skill or ability of a person to connect with other people's thoughts and emotions (Keum & Shin, 2016). Empathy is particularly important in the context of negotiations for multiple reasons. First, understanding emotions and thoughts of other parties in a negotiation helps parties better shape their communication. Second, research suggests that empathy is positively related to altruism, cooperation and perception of fairness in social interactions (Klimecki et al., 2016). Enhanced cooperation and perceptions of fairness in social interactions such as negotiations can lead to a win-win outcome. Perceived altruism among parties in a negotiation is also a key driver to the success of negotiations. Altruism is a behavior when people prioritize interests of other people before their own interests. Altruism can do wonders in a negotiation as parties who perceive altruistic from other parties might return the favor by enhancing cooperation and concluding negotiations harmoniously.

Empathy is essentially a reflection process wherein people connect to other people's feelings (affective) and experiences (cognitive) (Chopik et al., 2017). The affective component is applicable during negotiation meetings. In negotiation meetings, people representing parties might have different forms of emotional expressions based on stimuli presented to them in form of agenda and arguments. Showing empathy to emotional responses is essential in negotiations. Even though a party may disagree with rebuttals against arguments, showing empathy toward feelings of parties bringing up rebuttals can foster a sense of cooperation and mutual respect. There might be instances when some parties might bring a rebuttal to the table based on their personal experiences. Instead of denying the rebuttal outright, it is best to acknowledge and appreciate the experiences highlighted by other parties while at the same time prepare a counter rebuttal based on facts.

Law 9: Building Trust Reduces Indifferences between Parties

Trust is defined as "… sentiment, or expectation about an exchange partner's trustworthiness" (Moorman et al., 1993). Trust construction and destruction is a process and is highly relevant in negotiations due to interpersonal contact between people representing parties. Trust is the confidence that people have in interpersonal exchanges so that people on the other side of the table will behave consistently with expectations (Ba & Pavlou, 2002). The core purpose of a negotiation is to hold extensive discussions to resolve interpersonal differences about a variety of issues and reach a win-win outcome. If parties in a negotiation are perceived as not trustworthy, then it can have detrimental effects on the outcome of negotiations. First, arguments brought up by parties perceived as not trustworthy will attract further scrutiny and will jeopardize the successful and timely commencement of negotiation. Second, if some parties in a negotiation are perceived as not trustworthy then it will lead to further escalation of indifferences by lowered levels of cooperation (Simon, 2007).

Building trust is a process, and it relies on the propensity to trust among people involved in the interaction. Propensity to trust is general expectations of people about relative trustworthiness of people they interact with (Rotter, 1971). Propensity to trust is a belief and shapes people's initial intentions to build trust in other people (Ferguson & Peterson, 2015). Propensity to trust is an important variable when people interact with relatively unknown people (Rotter, 1971). In negotiations, if parties have a personal or business relationship then it is highly likely that the trust formation or destruction process is already complete which ultimately shapes how these parties behave in their interpersonal contact. On the hand, when parties negotiate with relatively unknown people, propensity to trust becomes evermore important. It is important for businesses to make sure that people representing their parties have high propensity to trust. Higher propensity to trust can initiate the process of building trust which will in turn be reciprocated with trust from other parties. This mutual process is key to reducing indifferences and building higher levels of cooperation.

Law 10: Irrationality of Other Party: Dig Deeper, You May Find Hidden Interest Sleeping Underneath!

Witnessing irrational behavior is not uncommon in negotiations. However, such behaviors might be completely rational and just to parties exhibiting such behaviors. There are instances when some parties are not able to communicate properly and do not elaborate on the reasoning behind their claims.

Under such circumstances, parties who are recipients of such communication might not be able to decipher as to why the concerned party is making the irrational behavior.

Parties can understand the motives behind irrational claims by utilizing the strategy of self-disclosure. Self-disclosure is the act of communicating personal information from one individual to another (Collins & Miller, 2004). Self-disclosure leads to interpersonal attraction between two individuals, as self-disclosure by one individual is associated with reciprocal self-disclosure from the other individual (Berg & Wright-Buckley, 1988). To understand what is going on in other people's mind, it is essential to start engaging in the practice of self-disclosure. Self-disclosure will in turn lead to reciprocal self-disclosure from other parties which will help uncover hidden motives and interests. Such hidden motives and interests can be addressed in negotiation meetings leading to successful outcomes that are perceived as equitable.

Chapter Summary

Negotiation is a social activity, and most entrepreneurs enter negotiations sometime in their entrepreneurial journey. However, entrepreneurs fail to realize that it is a process involving multiple people, and the success of negotiations relies on utilizing the right strategies. In this chapter, we have outlined 10 relevant laws of negotiations. The first law emphasizes the importance of agenda and priorities in negotiations. All parties in negotiation have their personal interests that they wish to be addressed. It is essential for entrepreneurs to enter negotiation meetings after carefully crafting their agenda and studying the agendas of other parties carefully. Negotiation meetings have time constraints and preparing in advance lowers the chance of unexpected delay.

The second law is about the importance of understanding the perspective of other parties in negotiation as well as recognizing their point of view. Such practices foster an environment of cooperation and mutual trust. Third law of negotiation is about the importance of preparing for unexpected and disastrous outcomes. Things may not always turn out as expected and entrepreneurs must expect the unexpected and be prepared for it. Laws 4 and 5 emphasize the importance of negotiation as a process and how entrepreneurs must not focus solely on the outcome. If the process is not adequate, the outcome may never be realized. Also, entrepreneurs must keep in mind that it is always wise to not hold assumptions and probe the intentions as well as interests of other parties in negotiation in detail.

Law 6 is about the timing of making offers in negotiations. An offer made too early or too late may have deleterious impact on outcomes. Not only the timing but using right strategy to shape the offer message is also important for achieving desired outcome. Being greedy and coming up with too many demands is never a wise choice. Law 7 emphasizes on negative outcomes of taking multiple interests at a time which might be perceived as an act of greed among other parties in negotiation. Building trust and empathy are keys to equitable outcome of negotiations and shape laws 8 and 9. Finally, law 10 explains why some parties engage in irrational behavior and how can entrepreneurs overcome irrational behavior and conclude negotiations harmoniously.

Key Terms

- Negotiation meeting
- Disastrous outcomes
- Negotiation process
- Offer timing
- Empathy
- Trust

Case

Zach is a 21-year-old senior at a university in Ohio. Zach's major is computer science, and he has a knack for coding. He was born in a small town near his university and grew up on a farm. Despite his background, he chose computer science as he was passionate about it since childhood. In his college years, Zach learned several programming languages and is now an expert in Python. During his free time, he loves developing applications and has multiple free applications on the apple store for people to download. One of Zach's friends advised him to start an entrepreneurial venture selling applications to small businesses. Even though he did not have entrepreneurial experience, Zach decided to go ahead and start a venture specializing in applications. Within the first few months of business, he was approached by a couple of businesses who wanted custom-built mobile applications for their existing websites. Zach setup a virtual meeting with one of the potential customers to discuss the details of their order.

Before the meeting, the potential customers sent a detailed list of desired functionalities for their mobile application. To Zach's surprise, they also sent existing offers from other suppliers of similar applications. The potential customers also mentioned the timeline within which they desired the mobile application to be delivered. All the information delivered to Zach took him by surprise as he believed that the negotiation meeting will be about him introducing the strengths and weaknesses of his command over application development. Zach was taken by surprise and had three days to prepare for the meeting. During these three days, he outlined how the application built by him will be superior to those offered by competitors. He also outlined how he planned to accomplish the task through a deliverable due every two weeks.

Zach finally entered the meeting with potential customers. Throughout the entire meeting, Zach made sure to be an active listener and understand the needs and communication style of the parties he was negotiating with. He did not offer his price till the very end of the meeting. Zach also made sure he did not overemphasize his capabilities and solely focused on addressing the needs of the customers. The potential customers mentioned the struggles they were facing with their website and the lack of a mobile application for their website. Throughout the meeting, Zach made sure to hear out the people on the other side of the table. Toward the end of the meeting, the potential customers decided to be customers and signed a contract for the price promised by Zach.

Q. 1 How did Zach prepare for the meeting? What lesson did he learn by starting the entrepreneurial venture in terms of negotiations?

Q. 2 Why did Zach not make an offer at the beginning of the meeting? What would have changed if he made a price offer at the beginning of the meeting?

Q. 3 How did Zach build trust among the potential customers?

References

Ba, S., and Pavlou, P. A. (2002). Evidence of the effect of trust building technology in electronic markets: Price premiums and buyer behavior. *MIS Quarterly*, 26(3), 243–268.

Berg, J. H., and Wright-Buckley, C. (1988). Effects of racial similarity and interviewer intimacy in a peer counseling analogue. *Journal of Counseling Psychology*, 35, 377–384.

Chopik, W. J., O'Brien, E., and Konrath, S. H. (2017). Differences in empathic concern and perspective taking across 63 countries. *Journal of Cross Culture Psychology*, 48, 23–38. DOI: 10.1177/0022022116673910.

Collins, N., and Miller, I. (2014). Self-disclosure and liking: A meta-analytic review. *Psychological Bulletin*, 116, 457–475.

Davison, W. P. (1983). The third-person effect in communication. *Public Opinion Quarterly*, 47(1), 1–15. DOI: 10.1086/268763.

Digman, J. M. (1990). Personality structure: Emergence of the five-factor model. *Annual Review of Psychology*, 41, 417–440.

Dunn, W. S., Mount, M. K., Barrick, M. R., and Ones, D. S. (1995). Relative importance of personality and general mental ability in managers' judgments of applicant qualifications. *The Journal of Applied Psychology*, 80(4), 500–509.

Ferguson, A. J., and Peterson, R. S. (2015). Sinking slowly: Diversity in propensity to trust predicts downward trust spirals in small groups. *Journal of Applied Psychology*, 100(4), 1012–1024.

Fishbein, M., and Ajzen, I. (1977). Belief, attitude, intention, and behavior: An introduction to theory and research. *Contemporary Sociology*, 6, 244.

Grahe, J. E., and Sheman, R. A. (2007). An ecological examination of rapport using a dyadic puzzle task. *Journal of Social Psychology*, 147, 453–475.

Greenbaum, R. L., Mawritz, M. B., and Eissa, G. (2012). Bottom-line mentality as an antecedent of social undermining and the moderating roles of core self-evaluations and conscientiousness. *The Journal of Applied Psychology*, 97(2), 343–359.

Kalyuga, S., Chandler, P., and Sweller, J. (1999). Managing split-attention and redundancy in multimedia instruction. *Applied Cognitive Psychology*, 13, 351–371.

Keum, S., and Shin, H. S. (2016). Rodent models for studying empathy. *Neurobiology Learning Memory*, 135, 22–26. DOI: 10.1016/j.nlm.2016.07.022.

Klimecki, O. M., Mayer, S. V., Jusyte, A., Scheeff, J., and Schönenberg, M. (2016). Empathy promotes altruistic behavior in economic interactions. *Science Report*, 6, 31961. DOI: 10.1038/srep31961.

Lewicki, R. J., and Stark, N. (1996). What is ethically appropriate in negotiations: An empirical examination of bargaining tactics. *Social Justice Research*, 9, 69–95. DOI: 10.1007/BF02197657.

Mayer, J. D., Salovey, P., Caruso, D. R., and Sitarenios, G. (2001). Emotional intelligence as a standard intelligence. *Emotion*, 1(3), 232–242. DOI: 10.1037/1528-3542.1.3.232.

Moorman, C., Deshpandé, R., and Zaltman, G. (1993). Factors affecting trust in market research relationships. *Journal of Marketing*, 57(1), 81–101.

Pruitt, Dean G. (1981). *Negotiation Behavior*. New York: Academic Press.

Rim, S., Amit, E., Fujita, K., Trope, Y., Halbeisen, G., and Algom, D. (2015). 'How words transcend and pictures immerse: On the association between medium and level of construal'. *Social Psychological and Personality Science*, Vol. 6, No. 2, pp. 123–130.

Rotter, J. B. (1971). Generalized expectancies for interpersonal trust. *American Psychologist*, 26(5), 443–452.

Simon, E. (2007). La confiance dans tous ses e´tats. *Revue Franc¸aisede Gestion*, 33(175), 83–94.

Sweller, J., van Merrienboer, J. J., and Paas, F. (1998). Cognitive architecture and instructional design. *Educational Psychology Review*, 10, 251–296.

Trope, Y., and Liberman, N. (2010). Construal-level theory of psychological distance. *Psychological Review*, 117(2), 440–463.

PART IV

NEGOTIATION AND WOMEN ENTREPRENEURS

Chapter 8

WOMEN ENTREPRENEURS
CAN LEAD NEGOTIATION

Learning Objectives

- Learn the importance of alternatives in negotiation
- Understand the importance of listening
- Explore techniques for effective listening
- Learn about the importance of power and how to enhance it
- Understand how to say "No" in a productive way

Opening Profile: Walmart Vendors

Walmart vendors are trained to treat their vendors in a variety of ways, depending on where you fit in their plan. This case shares the story of a vendor called Sarah who negotiated a win-win outcome with Walmart. Walmart, the world's largest retailer, sold $514.4 billion worth of goods in 2019. A partnership with Walmart is either the Holy Grail or the kiss of death, given the organization's single-minded focus on EDLP (everyday low pricing) and its ability to make or break suppliers. However, one's perspective may make a difference.

Sarah Talley (owner of Frey Farms) acquired a deep understanding of the Walmart culture while finding "new money" in the supply chain through innovative tactics.

For example, Frey Farms used school buses ($1,500 each) instead of tractors ($12,000 each) as a cheaper and faster way to transport melons to the warehouse.

Talley also was skillful at negotiating a coveted co-management supplier agreement with Walmart, showing how Frey Farms could share the responsibility of managing inventory levels and sales and ultimately save customers' money while improving their own margins.

Sarah Talley's key negotiation principles:

When you have a problem, when there's something you engage in with Walmart that requires agreement so that it becomes a negotiation, the first advice is to think in partnership terms and really focus on a common goal, for example, getting costs out and asking questions. Don't make demands or statements. Rather ask if you can do this better. If the relationship with Walmart is truly a partnership, negotiation to resolve differences should focus on long-term mutual partnership gains.

Don't spend time griping. Be problem solvers instead. Approach Walmart by saying, "Let's work together and drive costs down and product it so much cheaper you don't have to replace me because if you work with me I could do it better."

Generate Alternatives for the Counterpart

Women entrepreneurs must keep in mind and evaluate every possible factor that might alter the outcome of negotiation in their entrepreneurial endeavors. Isolating and evaluating every critical factor to the success of negotiation can be a difficult task. However, there are some practices that entrepreneurs in general can adopt when entering negotiations to maximize rewards and minimize risks. For example, Abramson (2005) outlined some good practices for negotiators to ensure favorable outcomes and minimize risks. The practices are asserting interests, presenting rational explanations, acting trustworthily and using objective standards. When asserting interests, negotiators must make sure to address the interests of all parties in the negotiation. This strategy is important for women entrepreneurs as they are perceived as communal and expected to be caring and upholding the welfare of others (Williams & Best, 1990). When women entrepreneurs engage in asserting the interests of other parties in negotiation it is in accordance with the expected behavior from women based on gender stereotypes. One way to assert the interests of other parties in negotiation is to generate alternatives for counterparts. When women entrepreneurs generate alternatives for counterparts, it is likely that counterparts will perceive the women entrepreneurs to be caring and compassionate of interests of other parties in negotiation.

While addressing the interests of other parties by generating alternatives, women entrepreneurs must ensure that they present rational explanations for alternatives. Merely presenting alternatives that may not be acceptable to other parties will not serve the true purpose of offering such alternatives. Women entrepreneurs must ensure to act ethically and build trust among other negotiations by presenting an array of alternatives that seem legitimate and do not merely serve the interests of women entrepreneurs alone. Such alternatives must meet objective standards and must not be vague and subjective. Objective standards in this context refer to offering alternatives that assert how the alternatives will objectively satisfy the needs of other parties in negotiation. An example of alternative meeting objective standard would be one that asserts how the entrepreneur will offer a specific price discount which will benefit other parties financially.

While crafting alternatives for other parties, it is common for entrepreneurs to utilize tactics and tricks. Tactics and tricks differ from each other. Tactics are persuasive attempts that are considered ethical whereas tricks are essentially considered unethical. Both tactics and tricks may deliver favorable outcomes for entrepreneurs in negotiation. An entrepreneur can deliberately overstate deliverables in their agenda, withhold critical information or threaten to terminate negotiations early if some of their demands are not met. Such practices are termed as tactics. On the other hand, tricks involve utilizing unethical practices such as outright lying about information presented in their agenda and offerings. Outright lying about critical information presented to other parties can have detrimental impact on trustworthiness of the party playing such tricks. For example, an entrepreneur may decide to present alternatives to other parties in a negotiation, but all the alternatives have false information except for one alternative. There might be a situation where the alternative with false information is appealing to other parties and in such instances, it is impossible for the presenter to deliver promises in this alternative as they are based on false information. Women entrepreneurs must be very careful when crafting alternatives and must always stay away from tricks.

Alternatives suggested by entrepreneurs are primarily persuasive messages which offer a variety of outcomes for other parties. Other parties in negotiation are primarily decision makers who will cognitively evaluate the alternatives and make a judgment whether such alternatives serve their needs adequately or not. The entrepreneurs proposing the alternatives have the choice of framing the messages in alternatives such as avoiding losses or promoting gains. Message decision framing is "Strategy that focus on the benefits of adopting a behavior (i.e., gain frame) or the losses of failing to adopt a behavior (i.e., loss frame)" (Rothman & Salovey, 1997). Research suggests that message decision framing has a significant impact on people's decision making wherein they are more sensitive to avoid accruing losses than making gains of similar value (Sokol-Hessner et al., 2009). For example, consumer exposed to loss frame messages were twice as likely to use credit cards that prevented losses as compared to credit cards that were promoted with gain frame messages as late as six months after message communication (Ganzach & Karashi, 1995).

There are multiple reasons why loss framing is more effective. First, under loss message framing conditions people search for more information and exert higher cognitive effort as compared to similar conditions with gain message framing (Ditto et al., 1998). When exposed to gain message framing, people are more likely to act carelessly and not pay attention to information (Denes-Raj & Epstein, 1994). Second, loss framing messages build trust in communicator (Evans & Beest, 2017). The evidence suggests that while crafting the alternatives, it is beneficial for entrepreneur to utilize loss framing. But the key question is which alternative must have loss framing? The answer is simple. The alternatives that the entrepreneurs wish to be accepted should have loss framing whereas other alternatives must have gain framing.

When crafting alternatives for counterparts, women entrepreneurs must also carefully understand their own culture and the culture of counterparts. Based on Hofstede (1991), culture has dimensions of power distance, individualism, uncertainty avoidance and masculinity/femininity. The uncertainty avoidance dimension of culture is important in this context. Certain cultures with unstable geopolitical environment have higher levels of uncertainty avoidance. People in such cultures lay more emphasis to risk aversion. Women entrepreneurs operating in such environment can enable this dimension of culture to their benefit. If they incorporate a sense of security and risk aversion in the alternatives they offer, it is likely that the strategy will most likely work in their favor.

Take Advantage of Your Strength Being an Active Listener

Listening is the cognitive activity of paying attention to and analyzing auditory information from other people (Bodie, 2012). The act of listening has beneficial outcomes in the context of marketing and entrepreneurship. Research suggests that when salespeople listen to their customers, it leads to improvement in relationship quality and customer satisfaction (Drollinger et al., 2006). When people listen to other people it fosters two-way communication (Bass & Riggio, 2006) which is essential to the success of negotiations. When people perceive that other people are listening to them, they are more willing to express their thoughts and expressions (Miller et al., 1983). In any negotiation it is essential for all parties to feel comfortable and share their thoughts and feelings. For women entrepreneurs, it is essential to understand the perceptions of other parties in negotiation. This can be achieved if the women entrepreneurs enable self-disclosure from other parties by listening to them. It is critical for women entrepreneurs to capture self-disclosure of other parties for multitude of reasons. First, if other parties are engaging in gender stereotypes, they will self-disclose them. Women entrepreneurs can neutralize them early in negotiation process and preventing negotiation failure. Second, if other parties are playing tricks or tactics in negotiation, then paying attention to their self-disclosure can potentially uncover such actions and neutralize their negative impact on outcomes of negotiation.

Negotiation is a social activity and at its core are the people who communicate with each other to reach a mutually desirable solution to a problem or opportunity. Listening is precursor to an environment that fosters intimacy between people and generates positive attitudes toward the person who pays attention to and listens to other people (Beukeboom, 2009). Intimacy between parties in a negotiation is essential as there is a chance that some people in the negotiations might be total strangers. Also, if there are women entrepreneurs present in negotiations, some male negotiators may not feel comfortable to openly express themselves by disclosing their thoughts, especially in male dominant cultures. Listening also enables empathy and lowers judgmental attitudes toward the listener (Rogers, 1975). Securing empathy and lowering judgmental attitudes are critical for the success of women entrepreneurs, especially in circumstances when other parties in negotiation are not familiar with women entrepreneurs.

People's emotional states are also impacted by their perception of whether other people are listening to them or not (Beukeboom, 2009). Emotions can be broadly classified as positively or negatively valenced (Russell & Barrett, 1999). Negative emotional states are sadness, fear, anger and so on. Positive emotional states are joy, happiness, excitement and so on. The affective events theory suggests that people's emotional states induced by certain events have an impact on their behavior in future events (Weiss & Cropanzano, 1996). For example, a person who is delighted by customer experience at a business is more likely to behave in a friendlier manner with other people. The results are also applicable in the context of negotiations. When women entrepreneurs listen to other parties in negotiation, it is likely to induce positive emotional states among members of such parties. Under the influence of positive emotions, negotiators on the other side of the table to women negotiators are more likely to shape judgments in favor of women negotiators.

We know that listening has positive outcomes, but how do people know that other people are listening to them? One of the ways to signal that a person is listening is through the usage of concrete language in communication (Packard & Berger, 2020). When people utilize concrete language, they actively utilize words that are very specific to an object or event (Semin & Fiedler, 1988). For example, while describing a meeting with someone, a person can use concrete language by saying they shook their hand. On the other hand, if the same event is described as just a meeting then the language is more abstract. In the context of negotiations, utilizing concrete language can do wonders for negotiators in multiple ways. First, it can successfully signal to other parties in negotiation that parties utilizing concrete language are listening to them. Second, it makes it easier for the listener to signal other parties as they can effectively utilize concrete information from conversations to shape their language. For women entrepreneurs, utilizing concrete language can do wonders. Concrete language is easier to construct based on facts picked up in conversations and details in agendas of negotiating parties. Women entrepreneurs can effectively utilize this strategy of concrete language even if there are language barriers or they are negotiating with parties who differ from them in terms of expertise or experience in the industry.

A very important strategy of good listening is active listening. Active listening is a set of behaviors that involve paying complete attention to other people, asking them open-ended questions and replying with personal thoughts and feelings (Nemec et al., 2017). By paying complete attention to other people, people eliminate any noise from their previous thoughts or environment from distracting them. This enables them to completely grasp what other people are saying to them. Asking open-ended questions and delivering conversation signals such as "go on," "aha" also help enable active listening. Asking open-ended questions signals to other people that the listener cares about and is curious to learn more. Also, this strategy enables the continuance of speaking-listening activity and encourages the speakers to reveal more about the topic of interest. Active listening can do wonders for women entrepreneurs as they might find themselves in negotiation situations where negotiations have stalled. There might be deadlocks as parties may not be able to reach a conclusion. As we already know that women are perceived as more communal and caring, they can engage in leadership roles by moving the conversations forward by engaging in active listening. Utilizing open-ended questions and signals can help them create an environment where all parties in negotiation will perceive that their opinion is being heard. The only way to break deadlock is by negotiating conversations and what better a tool than active listening by women entrepreneurs.

Not only is active listening helpful for women entrepreneurs in negotiating with external entities, but it also helps them build better manage communication and relationships between members of their ventures. We know that active listening enables members of organizations to cooperate with each other in a more efficient manner which in turn leads to the better financial outcome for the organizations (Brownell, 2008). When women entrepreneurs listen to members of their ventures, they are more likely to discover the strengths and weaknesses of the business. This knowledge is critical to shaping agendas before entering negotiations with external parties. Also, active listening by women entrepreneurs can help them make better decisions in negotiations which are dynamic in nature and evolve as the negotiations unfold. If the negotiators do not listen to the members of their ventures, then it is highly likely that they are unaware of critical information about their own organization, and it will prevent them from making quick decisions as negotiations unfold.

Concessions Are Good! Learn to Use Your Power Rather Than Relying Much on Concessions

Power is an interesting concept and is highly relevant in negotiations. In any relationship, a party has higher power if other parties depend on them (Emerson, 1962). In negotiations the negotiating parties may have access to alternatives when making critical decisions. Power in negotiation is contingent on the quality of alternatives available to a party; greater and better the alternatives, the higher power a party enjoys (Thibaut & Kelley, 1959). Parties in negotiation wish to achieve an outcome that serves the needs of every party. However, every party has the incentive to enhance their reward if possible. Parties who enjoy a larger number of better alternatives are more likely to witness a larger share of reward as compared to other parties in negotiation (Thibaut, 1968). It is intuitive that in a negotiation meeting, parties who enjoy higher levels of power will exercise their power and demand concessions. Threats to abandon negotiations and exercise access to alternatives are common tactics in negotiation. The parties who do not enjoy high levels of power do not have much choice but to offer concessions. To avoid situations like this it is essential for parties to improve their power in negotiations (Thompson, 1998).

Entrepreneurs can enhance their power by forming alliances with other people or entities. We know that access to resources is a precursor to power and the parties with higher access to resources enjoy higher levels of power. Alliances based on maximizing control over resources are called resource complementarities, and they create joint value for all parties in the alliance (Bouncken et al., 2020). This strategy is critical for women entrepreneurs as they have lower access to resources as compared to their male counterparts. In such cases, women entrepreneurs can form alliances with other women entrepreneurs wherein they complement each other's resources thereby enabling creating joint value in form of enhanced power. For example, let us assume Sasha is an artisan entrepreneur who exports handicrafts from her home country of Ukraine. Sasha regularly supplies to retailers all over the world but finds it challenging to negotiate with foreign buyers as they have access to similar handicrafts sold by other exporters in Ukraine. Her compromised power has forced her to offer products at paper-thin margins. However, Sasha realized that she specializes in a special form of embroidery which is created by artisans in a specific region of Ukraine. To increase her power in negotiations she decided to form an alliance of exporters who employ artisans crafting the specific art. Her endeavors succeeded as foreign buyers were no longer able to use their power and drive down prices. The reason for the change was the fact that the only place they could source the special art was through the alliance. The endeavor also had favorable outcome for the artisans who enjoyed much higher levels of wages and better work conditions as compared to pre alliance era.

We live in a world where economic, technological and geopolitical conditions change very fast. Such changes have an impact on the economy. Products or services go redundant because of the introduction of new technologies. Markets in some countries get eliminated overnight because of sanctions levied by government agencies. Such conditions call for entrepreneurs to engage in enhancing their power through dynamic capabilities. The theory of dynamic capabilities suggests that entities can increase their power by gaining and releasing resources based on evolving economic environment (Lavie, 2006). Women entrepreneurs can enhance their power in negotiations by evaluating and deploying their dynamic capabilities. They must realize that change is inevitable and must act in accordance with changing conditions and adjust their offerings which yield the most rewards.

Knowing When to Say "No" Is Crucial in Negotiation: A "Must" Learn Factor for Women Entrepreneurs to Strike Win-Win Deals

Women entrepreneurs face unique challenges in negotiations and one of them is to be able to assert dominance in negotiations by saying "No." This is a unique challenge for women as they are not perceived to be agentic and saying a direct "No" to an offer from a negotiating party is viewed as a violation of gender stereotypes among male counterparts (Eagly et al., 1992). But there are some situations that call for women entrepreneurs to say "No" to offers from negotiators on the other side of the table. One of the strategies to utilize in such situations is to engage in transparent self-disclosure. The self-disclosure is transparent because it involves truthful and honest disclosure of intentions to not accept the offer. Transparent self-disclosure also helps communicate exact details of why the offer is not acceptable. Women entrepreneurs can also engage in the strategy of tentative communication style. When people engage in tentative communication, they engage in using questions and disclaimers (Carli, 1990). Utilizing tentative communication styles helps build trust as compared to assertive communication style (Carli, 1990).

Chapter Summary

This chapter highlights innovative ways which women entrepreneurs can utilize to generate favorable outcomes for themselves and create a win-win solution for all parties in negotiation. It is very essential for women entrepreneurs to understand the importance of generating alternatives for the counterparts in negotiation. Generating alternatives for counterparts makes them feel that women entrepreneur cares for their needs and is not trying to maximize their personal gain. It is essential for women entrepreneurs to stay away from tricks in negotiation as they might diminish trust if uncovered. While shaping alternatives, women entrepreneurs must make sure to craft the desired alternative with loss framing where less desired alternative with gain decision framing. Active listening can do wonders for women entrepreneurs in negotiations. It can help build trust among parties in negotiation. Also, active listening within their own ventures enables women entrepreneurs to better understand the strengths and weaknesses of their venture. Ventures led by women can also be victims of low power in negotiations. Women negotiators can enhance their relative power in negotiations by forming alliances with other entrepreneurs who have access to critical resources. Also, they must incorporate dynamic capabilities in their strategy to best utilize changes in market conditions to their benefit. Finally, if offers from other parties in negotiation are not acceptable, they must also learn to say no but by utilizing tentative communication style.

Key Terms

- Alternatives
- Active listening
- Concessions
- Power

Case

Linda is a proud entrepreneur who lives in Illinois. Her entrepreneurial success dates back couple of years, and she has primarily focused on the arts and crafts industry. Last year, Linda decided to start a construction company and specializes in single-family homes. To initiate construction operations, she secured a loan from a local bank. Her first project is spread over 50 acres and comprises 100 single-family homes. Her father was a builder, so she has some experience in construction but lacks contacts in the industry to source contractors. She uses her father's network to contact local builders and sets up a meeting with a contractor who specializes in foundation work.

The contractors visit the site and work on formulating their estimates. Linda and contractors decide to meet in two weeks to discuss cost and timeline estimates. In the meantime, Linda decides to contact other foundation contractors and request them to provide their estimates for building foundations. Linda postpones the negotiation meeting with the first contractor for one week citing the reason that she needed more time on her end to evaluate the project. But the contractor delivers his estimate on the promised date. During this period, Linda studies the offers provided by other contractors and figures out that she can negotiate with the first contractor based on estimates from other contractors. She creates multiple alternatives for the contractor wherein she changes the brand of cement used in foundations. She enters the negotiations with the contractor and delivers her alternatives to the contractor. The contractor starts explaining the reasons they are commanding the highest price. Instead of brushing off their claims, she listens to the contractor and acknowledges the fact that they are offering the "good" price. She does not interrupt the contractor and lets them explain the superiority of their deliverables. When contractors were finished explaining, Linda explains to them that she has offers from multiple other contractors and coveys her best prices. The contractors reduce their price but still did not match Linda's price. She was tempted to say no to the contractor; however, she tells the contractor that she is not sure about the price as it did not fit her budget. To her surprise, the contractor agreed to close the deal at the price offered by Linda.

Q. 1   How did Linda generate alternatives for the contractor?
Q. 2   Did Linda use concrete language to signal that she is listening? If yes, how?
Q. 3   What made the contractor agree to Linda's final price?

References

Abramson, H. (2005). 'Problem-solving advocacy in mediations: A model of client representation'. *Harvard Negotiation Law Review*, Vol. 10, p. 103.

Bass, B. M., and Riggio, R. E. (2006). *Transformational Leadership* (2nd ed.). Mahwah, NJ: Lawrence Erlbaum Associates Publishers.

Beukeboom, C. J. (2009). When words feel right: How affective expressions of listeners change a speaker's language use. *European Journal of Social Psychology*, *39*, 747–756.

Bodie, G. D. (2012). 'Listening as positive communication'. *The Positive Side of Interpersonal Communication*, Chapter 7, pp. 109–125.

Bouncken, R. B., Fredrich, V., Kraus, S., and Ritala, P. (2020). Innovation alliances: Balancing value creation dynamics, competitive intensity and market overlap. *Journal of Business Research*, *112*, 240–247.

Brownell, J. (2008). Exploring the strategic ground for listening and organizational effectiveness. *Scandinavian Journal of Hospitality and Tourism, 8*, 211–229.

Carli, L. L. (1990). Gender, language, and influence. *Journal of Personality and Social Psychology, 59*(5), 941–951.

Denes-Raj, V., and Epstein, S. (1994). Conflict between intuitive and rational processing: when people behave against their better judgment. *Journal of Personality and Social Psychology, 66*, 819–829.

Ditto, P. H., Scepansky, J. A., Munro, G. D., Apanovitch, A. M., and Lockhart, L. K. (1998). Motivated sensitivity to preference-inconsistent information. *Journal of Personality and Social Psychology, 75*, 53–69.

Drollinger, T., Comer, L. B., and Warrington, P. T. (2006). Development and validation of the active empathetic listening scale. *Psychology & Marketing, 23*, 161–180.

Eagly, A. H., Makhijani, M., and Klonsky, B. G. (1992). "Gender and the evaluation of leaders: A meta-analysis": Correction to Eagly et al. *Psychological Bulletin, 112*(3), 557.

Emerson, R. M. (1962). Power-dependence relations. *American Sociological Review, 27*, 31.

Evans, A. M., and Beest, I. (2017). Gain-loss framing effects in dilemmas of trust and reciprocity. *Journal of Experimental Social Psychology, 73*, 151–163.

Ganzach, Y., and Karsahi, N. (1995). Message framing and buying behavior: A field experiment. *Journal of Business Research, 32*, 11–17.

Hofstede, G. (1991). *Cultures and Organizations: Software of the Mind.* London: McGraw-Hill.

Lavie, D. (2006). The competitive advantage of interconnected firms: An extension of the resource-based view. *Academy of Management Review, 31*, 638–658.

Miller, L. C., Berg, J. H., and Archer, R. L. (1983). Openers: Individuals who elicit intimate self-disclosure. *Journal of Personality and Social Psychology, 44*, 1234–1244.

Nemec, P., Spagnolo, A. C., and Soydan, A. S. (2017). Can you hear me now? Teaching listening skills. *Psychiatric Rehabilitation Journal, 40*, 415–417.

Packard, G., and Berger, J. A. (2020). How concrete language shapes customer satisfaction. *Journal of Consumer Research, 47*, 787–806.

Rogers, R. W. (1975). A protection motivation theory of fear appeals and attitude change. *The Journal of Psychology, 91*(1), 93–114.

Rothman, A. J., and Salovey, P. (1997). Shaping perceptions to motivate healthy behavior: the role of message framing. *Psychological Bulletin, 121*(1), 3–19.

Russell, J. A., and Barrett, L. F. (1999). Core affect, prototypical emotional episodes, and other things called emotion: Dissecting the elephant. *Journal of Personality and Social Psychology, 76*(5), 805–819.

Semin, G. R., and Fiedler, K. (1988). The cognitive functions of linguistic categories in describing persons: Social cognition and language. *Journal of Personality and Social Psychology, 54*, 558–568.

Sokol-Hessner, P., Hsu, M., Curley, N. G., Delgado, M. R., Camerer, C., and Phelps, E. A. (2009). Thinking like a trader selectively reduces individuals' loss aversion. *Proceedings of the National Academy of Sciences, 106*, 5035–5040.

Thibaut, J. W. (1968). The development of contractual norms in bargaining: Replication and variation. *Journal of Conflict Resolution, 12*, 102–112.

Thibaut, J. W., and Kelley, H. H. (1959). *The Social Psychology of Groups.* New York: John Wiley & Sons.

Thompson, L. (1998). 'A new look at social cognition in groups'. *Basic and Applied Social Psychology*, Vol. 20, No. 1, pp. 3–5.

Weiss, H. M., and Cropanzano, R. (1996). 'A theoretical discussion of the structure, causes and consequences of affective experiences at work'. *Research in Organizational Behavior*, Vol. 18, pp. 17–19.

Williams, J., and Best, D. L. (1990). *Sex and Psyche: Gender and Self Viewed Cross-Culturally*. London: Sage.

Chapter 9

WOMEN ENTREPRENEURS CAN WIN NEGOTIATION

Learning Objectives

1. To understand the role of culture in women entrepreneurship
2. Evaluate the negative impact of gender stereotypes
3. Understand how women entrepreneurs utilize social and psychological capital
4. To understand the importance of business networks for women entrepreneurs

Opening Profile: Time Warner Cable

Time Warner Cable reported a huge quarterly loss of television subscribers, the largest in its history: 306,000 of its 11.7 million subscribers had dropped the company, the *New York Times* reports. An impasse with television networks CBS over fees led to Time Warner blacking CBS out of millions of homes in New York, Los Angeles, and Dallas for a month during the summer of 2013.

The parties' ultimate agreement was viewed as a victory for CBS, which won a promise of significantly higher fees for its programming in the blacked-out cities, from about $1 per subscriber to $2, as well as the digital rights to sell its content to web-based distributors such as Netflix. Time Warner halted the blackout and conceded in large part because it feared a mass exodus of subscribers if the dispute interrupted the start of Monday night football on CBS.

Time Warner's disappointing news highlights why attempts to punish a negotiation counterpart into conceding often backfire. Time Warner's focus on the pain it was inflicting on CBS blinded it to the likelihood that it would suffer from the blackout at least as much. Rather than spurring agreement, such hardball tactics tend to escalate disputes and drive parties even farther apart.

Don't Take Things for Granted; It Will Cost You

Women are generally perceived to have lower power than men. The statement finds support from data provided by UN women, 2018. The data suggests that millions of primary school-aged girls are not able to attend primary schools. The same is not true for primary school-aged boys. UN women also highlight that there is a global gender pay gap of about 23 percent and women are also more likely to experience physical and sexual violence from their partners. At the beginning of the twenty-first century, it was estimated that 60 percent of the world's poor were females of a variety of ages (UNIDO, 2001). To overcome such high levels of inequality and poverty, women have chosen the path of entrepreneurship (Sutter et al., 2019). Unfortunately, the entrepreneurial journey and success for women have been anything but easy. We know that the success rate of entrepreneurial ventures initiated by women is significantly lower than similar ventures initiated by men (Radović-Markovíc, 2017). Women entrepreneurs face numerous challenges which are a consequence of reasons that are often overlooked. Some of the key barriers to the success of women entrepreneurs will be discussed in this section as it is important for women entrepreneurs to address these barriers that ultimately lead to successful entrepreneurial outcomes.

Women entrepreneurs are present worldwide, and a key determinant of their success is the culture of the society that they live and operate in. Culture is a "set of beliefs and values about what is desirable and undesirable in a society, with formal and informal practices that support those values" (Javidan & House, 2001). A culture can be collective or individualistic. In collective cultures, people value their close interconnected groups over personal achievements. On the other hand, an individualistic culture is more aligned toward chasing personal preferences and self-reliance. In collective cultures, women are the primary caregiver for their families and when they have entrepreneurial income, it is utilized to provide for their families (Ahl, 2006). They engage in entrepreneurial activities when their male partners are unable to provide for their families (Rindova et al., 2009). In other cases, they do it to satisfy personal needs of achievement or hobbies. In both the cases, women entrepreneurs face unique challenges, and things are somewhat easier for women in individualistic cultures.

In collective cultures, women are expected to behave in congruence with the expected norms of their individual social groups they belong. Forming an entrepreneurial venture might be viewed as a violation of collective norms of their group in some cultures. In some cultures, gender hierarchy is still prevalent, and women are expected to only take care of household chores; engaging in entrepreneurial activities is viewed as a man's job and might be perceived as an illegitimate activity for a woman to engage in (Marlow & McAdam, 2015). To overcome this barrier, women entrepreneurs must engage in negotiations with their male partners to demonstrate the need for their entrepreneurial venture. Sometimes, women ignore the importance of negotiations which ultimately leads to friction with male partners and a lower likelihood of initiation and success of their entrepreneurial ventures.

Cultures have also shaped gender roles which create unique challenges for women entrepreneurs. Gender roles are essentially embedded in a society's culture and affect women's personal and work life as in some cultures women may not be expected to be seen as breadwinners and their culture only approve of tasks that involve taking care of household duties (de Bruin et al., 2007). Women are also viewed as having communal characteristics whereas men are viewed to be more agentic. People with agentic behaviors are perceived as masculine and are expected to be independent and confident (Eagly & Johannesen-Schmidt, 2001). On the other hand, people with communal behaviors are viewed as feminine and are expected to be helping others and focus on maintaining relationships (Eagly & Johannesen-Schmidt, 2001). Such categorized gender roles create problems for women entrepreneurs as entrepreneurship is viewed as an agentic behavior that may not be expected from women. In western cultures, women have been able to successfully break the glass ceiling to some extent, but the challenge is still real for women entrepreneurs in the developing world. Women entrepreneurs often witness invisible psychological and mental barriers in the form of glass ceilings which are a result of gender roles entrenched in cultures. When women entrepreneurs want to participate shoulder to shoulder in the business world, they are perceived as a threat to the male leadership dominance in some cultures. Women entrepreneurs do have the required knowledge, skills and experience to perform at par with men in entrepreneurial conquest (Heilman & Chen, 2003). Despite their capabilities, they often face backlash from men when they violate their gender role expectancies.

The consequences of violation of gender roles are witnessed in the form of a higher rate of failure for women-led entrepreneurial ventures in general; in particular, higher failure rate for women-led entrepreneurial ventures when women are perceived as not having enough competence for the role; at the same time lower failure rate for male-led ventures even if they are perceived as not competent for leading the venture (Yang & Triana, 2019). The phenomenon finds support from the role congruity theory. The theory posits that gender roles create implicit assumptions among people about the value generated by male- or female-dominated leadership. Such assumptions are driven by expectations that different genders have different levels of competencies for tasks such as leading an entrepreneurial venture. Even if men do not have competencies to lead an entrepreneurial venture, they often get the benefit of doubt and are viewed as taking on an unfit role only to progress toward a better role in future (Simpson, 2004). On the other hand, when women entrepreneurs do not have core competencies for the job, they are slapped with penalties as people perceive that it was a mistake to let an incompetent woman lead the venture. Part of the reason for this phenomenon is that men usually have higher social status in most cultures than women (Ridgeway et al., 1994). Thus, for any woman entrepreneur, ignoring the importance of gender roles can be catastrophic. Women entrepreneurs must not take things for granted and must equip themselves with essential skills to overcome such situations.

The barriers to success of women in professional world have led to the rise of women empowerment movements across the world. Women empowerment is a process that allows women to act in an agentic manner and gain access to resources which are critical for their success (Kabeer, 1999). Acting in agentic manner has historically been viewed as a man's job. But it is essential for women to act in agentic manner to achieve empowerment. When a person acts in an agentic manner, they are perceived as self-confident, masculine and decision makers. If there is no women empowerment, then we will continue to witness the negative impact of gender roles and women entrepreneurs' likelihood of success will be perpetually discounted. Empowerment can be achieved at personal level or in relation to others (Duvendack et al., 2014). In both cases, the role of relationships that women have with other people is important. The concept of power is grounded in social relationships that people have with other people. Thus, to achieve empowerment for themselves women must engage in extensive negotiations with people who matter in terms of their entrepreneurial success. While negotiating, women must make sure to act in an agentic manner to achieve empowerment and must speak up for their rights, interests and needs. Women empowerment can also be achieved through women entrepreneurial role models. Role models are "individuals whose behaviors, personal styles, and specific attributes are emulated by others" (Shapiro et al., 1978, p. 52). In the last few decades, role models for successful women entrepreneurs have emerged who have defied gender stereotypes and broken the predisposition that women entrepreneurs cannot act in agentic manner. An iconic role model for women entrepreneurs is Oprah Winfrey. For decades, Oprah has defied gender stereotypes and challenged the assumption that women cannot achieve their entrepreneurial goals. Thus, we can conclude that gaining empowerment and acting in agentic manner is essential for the success of women entrepreneurs. Failure to achieve empowerment by agentic behaviors will most likely lead to continuance of gender stereotypes.

The advancement in digital technologies during the last few decades has significantly enhanced the entrepreneurial possibilities (Castells, 2010). The internet has enabled women entrepreneurs to act in agentic way like never. For example, the online shopping website Etsy.com has afforded the opportunity to women artisan entrepreneurs to sell directly to consumers. This makes us assume that an online environment would naturally empower women entrepreneurs. However, a study by Dy et al. (2017) suggests that contrary to intuition, women entrepreneurs who face gender stereotypes present in offline environments are likely to witness the negative impacts of such stereotypes in online environments as well. This phenomenon raises questions about the importance and severity of gender stereotypes in a world that is increasingly relying on digital technologies. Women entrepreneurs must not take things for granted and be prepared for negative consequences of gender stereotypes in any kind of environment.

Know Your Value in the Negotiating Table

Negotiations are key to the survival of entrepreneurial ventures. The reason for claim is that the resources available to entrepreneurs are limited leading them to negotiate generating favorable outcome for themselves. Women entrepreneurs and men entrepreneurs differ in terms of possible outcomes of their negotiations, with women entrepreneurs not able to generate favorable outcomes for themselves. The reason behind such undesirable circumstances is that women face prejudice and biases because of gender stereotypes and are not able to generate rent for themselves in negotiations.

Negotiations put capabilities of an entrepreneur to test and an entrepreneur who does not bring the best to table may not succeed in the long run. In general, successful entrepreneurs have higher levels of self-efficacy, perseverance, opportunity recognition, human and social capital as well as social skills (Markman & Baron, 2003). Self-efficacy is the belief that an entrepreneur has in themselves to complete a task. For female entrepreneurs, it is essential to have high levels of self-efficacy. If women entrepreneurs do not believe in themselves to push their position in a negotiation, then it is highly likely that other parties in negotiation will easily utilize stereotypes to generate rent only for themselves in negotiation. Most entrepreneurs face some sort of setbacks in their entrepreneurial journey. However, women entrepreneurs must realize that other parties in negotiation might use some setbacks to test the perseverance of women entrepreneur. Handling setbacks in a calm composed way and learning from such setbacks is essential in negotiation.

Negotiation is a social activity as it involves multiple parties who are trying to reach a mutually beneficial solution. Each party wants to influence the other party to achieve a desired outcome for themselves. In such circumstances, the concept of social capital is highly relevant. Social capital does lead to opportunities available to an entity because of who the entity is connected to. Such connections can be influential organizations, people and so on. For women entrepreneurs it is essential for them to evaluate their social capital and utilize it to the full for their benefit. Women entrepreneurs can take on agentic behaviors by utilizing their social capital in negotiations which can eventually lead to higher levels of power enjoyed.

Social capital varies among different cultures. Different cultures value different attributes of social connections. For instance, in the north African country of Tunisia, women entrepreneurs enjoy the benefits of social capital of marital status and wasta (Baranik et al., 2018). Women entrepreneurs in Tunisia enjoy the social capital of marital status as marriage provides them with resources through their spouse. Wasta refers to the ability of achieving goals by knowing influential people (Berger et al., 2015). Women entrepreneurs who wish to engage in negotiations can utilize wasta to their benefit. Even if they have lower power than their male negotiators, they can make up for the negative impact of stereotypes by utilizing associations with influential people which will help them achieve better outcomes in negotiations.

There might be instances when women entrepreneurs might feel that they do not have adequate resources or capabilities as compared to other parties in a negotiation. In such situations, women entrepreneurs must engage in the strategy of bricolage. Bricolage simply means making do with what is available. It has also been defined as "making do by applying combinations of resources at hand to new problems and opportunities" (Baker & Nelson, 2005). To achieve bricolage in a negotiation, women entrepreneurs need to rely on their psychological capital. Psychological capital is a distinct concept from social capital and is concentrated on the abilities afforded to the entrepreneur based on their personal qualities or traits. It is defined as "having confidence (self-efficacy) to take on and put in the necessary effort to succeed at challenging tasks; making a positive attribution (optimism) about succeeding now and in the future; persevering toward goals and, when necessary, redirecting paths to goals (hope) in order to succeed; and when beset by problems and adversity, sustaining and bouncing back and even beyond (resiliency) to attain success" (Luthans et al., 2007).

Negotiation is a challenging task that requires all participants, especially the ones with lower power, to utilize their social and psychological capital for maximized favorable outcomes for themselves. For every decision to be made in a negotiation, each party engages in a cognitive process of evaluating the outcome of their decisions and if such outcomes can be achieved or not. The claim finds support from expectancy theory (Lawler, 1973) which emphasizes this two-step process of motivations toward deciding to engage in a particular task. For women entrepreneurs, evaluating favorable outcomes of their decisions and the feasibility of such outcomes is important. As women entrepreneurs have access to fewer resources and power as compared to their male counterparts, they must act toward evaluating every decision carefully in negotiations and utilizing their social and psychological capital to maximize the possibility of favorable outcomes for themselves.

Like other entrepreneurs, ventures initiated by women must ensure two-way communication with all the stakeholders. In negotiation settings, parties on the other side of the negotiating table are stakeholders as well. In many cases, women entrepreneurs encounter these stakeholders over multiple negotiations spread over months or years. Thus, it is essential that women entrepreneurs manage communication and relationship with such stakeholders. Stakeholder management is beneficial for women entrepreneurs as research suggests that stakeholder management is positively related to women entrepreneurial innovations (Nair, 2020). Stakeholder management is "a process of identifying, analyzing, communicating, decision-making, and the other activities involved in managing stakeholders" (Nair, 2020). Stakeholder management by women entrepreneurs can act as a form of communal behavior on behalf of the entrepreneurs. Such management will also help build long-term relationships with people who will be seen on the other side of negotiation table in future.

According to Nair (2020), stakeholder engagement process is a three-step process. The first step is about creating a stakeholder engagement plan. The plan is about identifying who the stakeholders are, what are their strengths and weaknesses relative to personal strengths and weaknesses, means to communicate and build relationships with these stakeholders. The second step in process is to develop stakeholder engagement strategy. The strategies adopted are based on the women entrepreneurs' social and psychological capital. Finally, the third step is strategic engagement process which is all about building trust and relationships with stakeholders based on effective communication. Thus, the key takeaway from the concept of stakeholder engagement is that it is essential for women entrepreneurs to have a deeper understanding and a mutually trustworthy relationship with the negotiators on the other side of the table. This strategy helps women entrepreneurs generate favorable outcome for themselves and simultaneously generate value for all parties in negotiation.

Strong Network Is Net-Worth in Negotiation

Entrepreneurship is a social process and involves extensive communication and negotiation with entities external to the entrepreneurial venture. As discussed in the previous sections, culture plays a vital role in shaping the expectancies of women entrepreneurs under the influence of gender roles. Such expectancies are also influenced by social structures of the culture in which the women entrepreneur operate in. Social structures are important for women entrepreneurs as they have a significant influence on the outcomes of behaviors of women entrepreneurs.

Social structures are "supraindividual phenomena with the attributes, attitudes, and behavior of people explained according to individuals' position within wider social relations" (Lent, 2020). For women entrepreneurs it is essential to recognize the impact of social structures and shape their behaviors which are most likely to align with expectancies in their social structures. There is an old saying "if you cannot beat them, join them." The same principle applies in this scenario as the women entrepreneurs have much less power than men and to achieve favorable outcomes for themselves, they must modify their behaviors based on social structures they operate in. Social structures have unique set of implicit and mutually agreed upon set of rules. Such rules determine what is acceptable and not acceptable. In a negotiation, women entrepreneurs can utilize such rules to their benefit and enhance their social capital only if they are cognizant of the rules and follow them.

Women entrepreneurs like their male counterparts conduct business with different external entities and sometimes such business transactions end up shaping relationships between the relationship partners. Such relationships are a result of negotiations and over time they are reinforced by mutual trust leading to a group of entities (businesses and entrepreneurs) that can be called a business network. Business networks are beneficial for entrepreneurs as they create win-win situation for all parties in the network (Khvatova et al., 2016). Business networks can do wonders for women entrepreneurs. First, they help lower the negative impact of gender stereotypes by building relationships between women entrepreneurs and other businesses. Second, business networks help women entrepreneurs by lowering the intensity and frequency of negotiations required to conduct business with entities external to their venture.

Women entrepreneurs can increase the size of their business networks through the process of socialization. Socialization involves putting in the effort to build personal relationships with external entities that they negotiate with. While socializing, they must engage in behaviors for themselves to overcome the glass ceiling, build trust and reduce the impact of gender stereotypes. Women are perceived as more communal, and they are expected to have concern for others, tenderness and expressiveness. Such expectancies might help build their business networks if they utilize the combination of both agentic and communal behaviors. The communal behaviors will help them achieve a foot in the door to business networks and agentic behaviors will help them achieve desired negotiation outcomes for their entrepreneurial ventures.

Chapter Summary

Entrepreneurial ventures led by women are less successful than similar ventures led by men. The reason for such a phenomenon is deeply rooted in cultures. Different cultures have different expectations from women. In some cultures, women are expected to take care of their household duties and bread-winning activities like entrepreneurship are considered a man's job. However, women still engage in entrepreneurial ventures to provide financially for their families when the male partners fail to do. Starting an entrepreneurial venture and making it successful are two different things. The chapter discusses barriers that women face in their entrepreneurial ventures and how they can overcome them.

The most critical barrier faced by women entrepreneurs is that of gender stereotypes. Women are perceived as more communal whereas men are perceived as more agentic. Entrepreneurship is an agentic activity that demands leadership, confidence and decision making. When women take on entrepreneurial roles, it is perceived as a defiance of their prescribed gender role. Women entrepreneurs can overcome the barrier of gender roles by building and utilizing their social and psychological capital. Social capital is built by having connection with influential people or organizations whereas psychological capital is gained by personal traits and qualities.

For women entrepreneurs, business networks matter a lot. Along with business networks, women entrepreneurs also benefit from social networks they are part of. Such networks help women entrepreneurs lower the negative impact of stereotypes and drive them closer to success in their entrepreneurial journey.

Key Terms

- Gender stereotypes
- Women empowerment
- Social capital
- Psychological capital
- Business networks

Case

Latika lives with her husband and three children in rural parts of Rajasthan, India. Latika's husband works for a nearby factory and is the sole breadwinner of the family. They live a modest life, and their needs are met by wages of Latika's husband. Due to unforeseen market conditions, Latika's husband loses his job and can no longer provide for the family. As a result of the financial hardship, Latika decides to start a business selling crafts made in her area on an online shopping website.

She had saved up some money in the past and uses the limited capital to start a small entrepreneurial venture on a popular arts and crafts website. Her products interest consumers and they start selling like hotcakes. Things take a sharp turn for her when her husband and other family members find out about her entrepreneurial venture. Unfortunately, she is asked to shut down the business as her husband and family feel that earning livelihood is her husband's job. Instead of engaging in revolt, Latika enters into a negotiation with her husband and family members. She offers a solution where her husband takes on a partner role with her in the entrepreneurial venture. Her solution is accepted by the family and her husband.

Her business grows fast which creates another challenge for Latika. She must soon ramp up her production or she will fall short of delivery deadlines for orders. To increase the production, she needs access to additional capital and labor. To overcome the barrier, she decides to partner with a local supplier of unfinished goods. Sourcing unfinished goods solves the problem as they can be easily finished at her facility, and she does not need additional capital. She meets with the potential supplier of unfinished goods, but the suppliers give her a hard time claiming that they are not sure whether they can trust her as they have never done business with her before. To overcome this barrier, she utilizes her social network and connects with friends of the supplier. Based on recommendations of numerous people, the supplier agrees to sell to Latika's business despite the lack of credibility of Latika's business.

Q. 1   How does Latika face gender stereotype?
Q. 2   How did she overcome the negative impact of stereotype?
Q. 3   How did Latika use her social and psychological capital?
Q. 4   How important were social and business networks to survival of Latika's business?

References

Ahl, H. (2006). Why research on women entrepreneurs needs new directions. *Entrepreneurship Theory and Practice* 30(5), 595–623.

Baker, T., and Nelson, R. E. (2005). Creating something from nothing: Resource construction through entrepreneurial bricolage. *Administrative Science Quarterly* 50(3), 329–366.

Baranik, L. E., Gorman, B., and Wales, W. J. (2018). What makes muslim women entrepreneurs successful? A field study examining religiosity and social capital in Tunisia. *Sex Roles* 78, 208–219.

Berger, R., Silbiger, A., Herstein, R., and Barnes, B. R. (2015). Analyzing business-to-business relationships in an Arab context. *Journal of World Business* 50, 454–464. DOI: 10.1016/j.jwb.2014.08.004.

Castells, M. (2010). *The Rise of the Network Society*. Chichester: Wiley-Blackwell.

de Bruin, A., Brush, C. G., and Welter, F. (2007). Advancing a framework for coherent research on women's entrepreneurship. *Entrepreneurship Theory and Practice* 31, 323–339.

Duvendack, M., Palmer-Jones, R., and Vaessen, J. (2014). Meta-analysis of the impact of microcredit on women's control over household decisions: Methodological issues and substantive findings. *Journal of Development Effectiveness* 6(2), 73–96. DOI: 10.1080/19439342.2014.903289.

Dy, A. M., Marlow, S., and Martin, L. (2017). A web of opportunity or the same old story? Women digital entrepreneurs and intersectionality theory. *Human Relations* 70, 286–311.

Eagly, A. H., and Johannesen-Schmidt, M. (2001). The leadership styles of women and men. *Journal of Social Issues* 57, 781–797.

Heilman, M. E., and Chen, J. J. (2003). Entrepreneurship as a solution: The allure of self-employment for women and minorities. *Human Resource Management Review* 13(2), 347–364. DOI: 10.1016/S1053-4822(03)00021-4.

Javidan, M., and House, R. J. (2001). Cultural acumen for the global manager: Lessons from project GLOBE. *Organizational Dynamics* 29, 289–305.

Kabeer, N. (1999). Resources, agency, achievements: Reflections on the measurement of women's empowerment. *Development and Change* 30(3), 435–464.

Khvatova, T., Block, M., Zhukov, D., and Lesko, S. (2016). How to measure trust: The percolation model applied to intra-organizational knowledge-sharing networks. *Journal of Knowledge Management* 20(5), 918–935.

Lawler, E. E. (1973). *Motivation in Work Organizations*. Monterey, CA: Brooks/Cole Publishing Co.

Lent, M. (2020). Everyday entrepreneurship among women in Northern Ghana: A practice perspective. *Journal of Small Business Management* 58, 777–805.

Luthans, F., Youssef, C. M., and Avolio, B. J. (2007). *Psychological Capital: Developing the Human Competitive Edge*. Oxford, UK: Oxford University Press.

Markman, G. D., and Baron, R. A. (2003). Person-entrepreneurship fit: Why some people are more successful as entrepreneurs than others. *Human Resource Management Review* 13, 281–301. DOI: 10.1016/S1053-4822(03)00018-4.

Marlow, S., and McAdam, M. (2015). Incubation or induction? Gendered identity work in the context of technology business incubation. *Entrepreneurship Theory and Practice* 39(4), 791–816. DOI: 10.1111/etap.2015.39.issue-4.

Nair, S. R. (2020). The link between women entrepreneurship, innovation and stakeholder engagement: A review. *Journal of Business Research* 119, 283–290.

Radović-Marković, M. (2017). Female entrepreneurship: Theoretical approaches. *Journal of Women's Entrepreneurship and Education* 1–2, 1–9.

Ridgeway, C. L., Johnson, C. J., and Diekema, D. (1994). External status, legitimacy, and compliance in male and female groups. *Social Forces* 72, 1051–1077.

Rindova, V., Barry, D., and Ketchen, D. J. (2009). Entrepreneuring as emancipation. *Academy of Management Review* 34, 477–491.

Shapiro, E., Haseltine, F., and Rowe, M. (1978). Moving up: Role models, mentors, and the "patron system.". *Sloan Management Review* 6(1), 19–47.

Simpson, R. (2004). Masculinity at work: The experiences of men in female dominated occupations. *Work, Employment and Society* 18, 349–368.

Sutter, C., Bruton, G. D., and Chen, J. (2019). Entrepreneurship as a solution to extreme poverty: A review and future research directions. *Journal of Business Venturing* 34(1), 197–214. DOI: 10.1016/j.jbusvent.2018.06.003.

UNIDO. (2001). *Women Entrepreneurship Development in Selected African Countries*. Vienna, AT: United Nations Industrial Development Organization.

Yang, T., and del Carmen Triana, M. (2019). Set up to fail: Explaining when women-led businesses are more likely to fail. *Journal of Management* 45, 926–954.

PART V

CULTURAL DYNAMICS AND NEGOTIATION

Chapter 10

CULTURE DIFFERENCES IMPACT NEGOTIATION: EMBRACE IT!

Learning Objectives

- To understand what is culture and how does it impact negotiations
- Evaluate the differential impact of cross-cultural negotiations on outcomes
- Understand the role of communication in negotiations
- Get familiar with self-serving biases in cross-cultural negotiations
- Evaluate how emotions shape outcomes of negotiations

Opening Profile: The Free Trade Agreement between Canada and United States

On October 3, 1987, the Free Trade Agreement (FTA) was signed by representatives of Canada and the United States after two strenuous years of intense negotiations. Canada could be described as a medium-sized economy. Its population is one-tenth the size of the United States, which is considered an economic superpower in comparison. More than 75 percent of its exports go to the United States making the United States Canada's prime trading partner. By contrast, the United States was exporting less than 20 percent of its products to Canada.

A Royal Commission concluded that Canada's only means to achieve this stability was to engage in an open free trade partnership with the United States.

The problem was that the United States wasn't especially interested in such a free trade partnership agreement.

The first step that Canada took was in the form of preparation by developing a succinct plan. A chief negotiator, Simon Reisman, was appointed by the Canadian prime minister himself. He established an ad-hoc organization called the trade negotiations office which reported directly to the Canadian Government Cabinet and had access to the highest levels of bureaucracy. It established in no uncertain terms their negotiation goals and objectives which included a strong dispute resolution mechanism that the Canadians felt was vitally important to their success.

In contrast, the United States did not consider the FTA to be especially important and let Canada do all the initial work. The only reason why the US Congress even considered the FTA proposal was that they liked the idea of a bilateral approach to trade and were tired of the previous mechanism that failed to settle a host of trade dispute irritants between the two countries known as GATT.

Strong differences in interests and approaches dogged the negotiations. The Canadians used every advantage available including the use of Summit negotiation meetings between the leaders of both countries to emphasize their concerns at every opportunity. Yet, the political powers in the United States dragged their feet to such an extent that the Canadian negotiators walked away from the talks to express their displeasure. This put some heat on the US administrators to the extent that US Treasury Secretary Baker took over the negotiations.

The FTA between the two countries created the largest bilateral trade relationship in the world. Canada achieved its objectives because of its detailed planning and the intense focus of its negotiating team despite the asymmetry in power between the two nations.

(This case study shows how a weaker negotiating partner can successfully use power negotiation to win a good agreement with a stronger negotiating partner. There are many occasions when a smaller company will want to form a negotiation partnership with a larger organization to further its business objectives. There are two hurdles that the smaller company might have to overcome to succeed in the negotiation process. The first problem is to get the larger organization's attention as they may express little to no interest in the partnership. The second problem revolves around the prickly issue of negotiating from a much weaker power base. There exists the danger that the smaller party's business goals aren't overwhelmed by the more powerful negotiating partner during the negotiation process.)

Cultural Factors and Cognitive Dynamics

Social interactions among entrepreneurs are a key characteristic of negotiation meetings. Negotiation meetings take place over a period that lead to repeat and stable patterns of social interactions (Brett et al., 2005). An important variable that shapes the process and outcome of such interactions is variation in cultures of parties partaking in negotiations. Culture is "socially shared knowledge structure, or schema, that guides the interpretation of incoming stimuli and subsequent outgoing reactions" (Triandis, 1972). Culture can have an impact on how people evaluate situations and behaviors (Cranavale, 1995); thus, it plays a crucial role in negotiations. The role of culture in negotiations is ever more important when negotiating parties do not share common cultures. People face issues when they interact with people from different cultures such as they have hard time interacting, understanding and evaluating the thoughts and opinions of others (Inman et al., 2014). So, what exactly is cultural difference and how does it impact negotiation outcomes? Cultural difference is the level of difference that people perceive in terms of race, religion, language and norms entrenched in societies as compared to their own subjective evaluation of self (Ghemawat, 2001). Higher levels of cultural differences can have detrimental negative impacts in negotiations. Negotiators who perceive higher levels of cultural differences among other parties are prone to rely on stereotypes and mental shortcuts while making inferences and judgments. Also, negotiators are likely to feel that negotiations are much more a difficult task in cross-cultural negotiations which in turn can inhibit them from focusing on the core issues that need to be discussed in negotiations.

Cultural differences hurt the outcomes of negotiations in different ways. Instances when cultural differences hurt outcomes of negotiations happen when negotiators from different cultures rely on the assumptions that customs practiced in their culture are also prevalent in cultures of their negotiation partners. For example, it is customary in American culture to be humorous and address other people as "funny" and "hilarious." Casual conversations in American culture often involve people addressing other people as "characters." However, engaging in such behaviors can have disastrous outcomes in eastern cultures which do not rely on assumption that it is ok to be funny and casual in interpersonal communication. Addressing people as "funny" or "characters" might be taken seriously and negotiation partners from eastern cultures might perceive such comments seriously. When such comments are taken seriously, negotiation partners from eastern cultures are likely to perceive that their North American counterparts are making fun of them, leading to retaliatory behaviors.

Eastern and western cultures differ in multitude of ways, and it is not possible to summarize all possible differences due to possible internal variance within these cultures. Although it is not possible to be cognizant of all the differences, but it is always helpful to be socially aware of some key differences while entering negotiations. Social awareness is the degree of being aware of other people's perspectives and paying attention to such perspectives (McGinn et al., 2004, p. 334). Failure of being socially aware might result in negotiators from other cultures categorizing socially unaware partners as

their enemies. Research suggests that negotiators often categorize their negotiation partners as friends or enemies (Hofstede, 2001). The last thing a negotiator wants is to be categorized as an enemy. For example, it is customary in
some cultures to wear clothing with flags of different countries. Such behavior
is considered offensive or even illegal in some countries. Some people also try
to signal their social awareness by dressing up in traditional clothing from
other cultures. The visit of Canadian prime minister Justin Trudeau to India
is a great example of negative evaluation of behaviors of the prime minister
by the Indian public. Justin Trudeau visited India in 2018 and based on an
article published in the *New York Times*, Trudeau's efforts to overdress in traditional Indian clothing was perceived as cultural condescension (Dan Bilefsky,
2018). It is pretty evident that Trudeau did not wear traditional Indian attire
to condescend Indian people, yet such efforts led to a disastrous outcome with
many negatively valenced posts going viral on Twitter at the time.

Understanding differences in eastern and western cultures is extremely
important for entrepreneurs. First, there might be situations where entrepreneurs might have to source products or services from other countries and the
impact of cultural difference between the entrepreneur and their suppliers
will play a role in outcomes of negotiations. Second, as countries become
increasingly diverse, there is also a possibility that workforce within ventures
led by entrepreneurs will be culturally diverse. It is critical for entrepreneurs
to have the necessary cognitive skills enabling them to successfully understand and negotiate with the culturally diverse workforce.

One of the key differentiating factors among cultures is the role of context.
People from different cultures vary in terms of their utilization of context in
negotiations. Some negotiators utilize high context in their negotiations, and
they tend to be indirect by utilizing context to convey messages to other parties; negotiators who utilize low context in negotiations tend to rely on explicit
verbal messages to convey their thought and feelings to other parties in negotiations (Adair, 2003). Western cultures such as the United States can be
classified as low-context culture, whereas eastern cultures such as Japan are
primarily high-context culture (Hall, 1971). Entrepreneurs from either high-
or low-context cultures must understand how this differentiator can impact
the perceptions of other parties in negotiations. For example, let us assume
that Tina is an entrepreneur from Chicago who travels to China to source
customized products for her upcoming clothing brand. She visits a clothing
manufacturer who agrees to manufacture for her. But Tina wants to negotiate
on pricing and delivery schedules before she formally places an order. As the
negotiations unfold, Tina is very direct and sets forth her expectations one by
one. On the other hand, representatives of the Chinese manufacturer listen
to Tina and are perplexed by the one-sided demands of their potential client.

The representatives address each demand by giving examples of how they have had similar demands in past and how they were met. As the negotiations progress, Tina is confused and feels that her demands have been ignored. At the same time, the representatives of the manufacturer feel that Tina is being too bossy and is not paying any attention to their perspectives. The negotiation meeting is inconclusive, and Tina decides to meet other suppliers feeling she wasted her time negotiating with a supplier who was not interested in doing business with her. This scenario is an example of how the difference in low- and high-context cultures can create misconceptions among negotiation partners leading to early termination of negotiation without any concrete outcome.

Eastern and western cultures also differ in terms of individualism and collectivism. Western cultures are more individualistic wherein people construe their personal self as detached from other people and focus solely on their individual attributes such as achievements and abilities (Markus & Kitayama, 1991). On the contrary, people in collectivist cultures view themselves as connected to others with less emphasis on personal achievement and abilities (Markus & Kitayama, 1991). Individualistic cultures are marred by the self-serving biases of fairness, wherein people serve themselves by standing out from the crowd (Heine et al., 1999) and showcase the individual self as relatively better than other people (Markus & Kitayama, 1991). Research suggests that people with self-serving bias of fairness are more likely to feel that they are generally fairer in their actions than others (Messick et al., 1985), are more successful and competent (Urban & Witt, 1990) and less likely to attribute failures to themselves Sedikides, et al. (1998). Such bias in individualistic cultures may not always be bad and people with such bias may be successful in negotiations that do not involve negotiators from collectivistic cultures. When cross-cultural negotiations do happen, self-serving bias of fairness can cause multitude of issues. Negotiators from collectivist cultures might perceive negotiators from individualistic cultures as selfish, outspoken and boastful. Such perceptions are likely to cause disruption in negotiations as negotiators from collectivist cultures might also sense that they are being bullied by negotiators from individualistic cultures. Simultaneously, negotiators from collectivist cultures might engage in behaviors that may not make sense to individualistic negotiators. People from collectivist culture view their personal selves as connected to others and are more likely to shape their thoughts with other people in mind. Such thoughts will ultimately lead to conversations that might sound relatively strange to negotiators from individualistic cultures creating a sense of confusion while judging the motives of collectivist negotiators.

No two people are the same, and the same rule applies to people from different cultures. Not only are cultures different, but people within different cultures have their individual differences. No matter the culture, it is essential for an entrepreneur to have the necessary cognitive skills to be able to judge deception from other parties in negotiation. Deception is nothing more than misrepresentation of emotions and critical information (Gaspar et al., 2015). When parties enter negotiations, they face the challenge of information asymmetry (Schweitzer & Hsee, 2002). Information asymmetries are situations where negotiating parties lack access to critical information that might be private to other parties in the negotiation process. Deception does not happen because parties withhold private information; it happens when they misrepresent information or their emotions. In short, they engage in outright lying behavior. But how do entrepreneurial negotiators detect deception in negotiations? Research suggests that "people with a pro-self-motivation are more likely to use deception than those with a prosocial motivation" (Steinel, 2015). The concept of pro-self motivation relates to individualism wherein people are more likely to focus on themselves as opposed to viewing themselves as a part of group. So, does that mean that negotiators from individualistic cultures are more likely to utilize deception? The answer to the question is yes and no. Individualistic negotiators may engage in deceptive practices as they are more likely to overstate their personal achievements and offers they have for other parties in negotiation. To avoid inference of malicious intent it is essential for negotiators from individualistic cultures to be respectful of perspectives of negotiators from collectivistic cultures and engage in a balanced manner by laying balanced emphasis on themselves and on signaling a bond with others. This can be achieved by actively listening to others, agreeing with others on some aspects and so on.

Negotiators are people who come from a variety of cultures, and they vary in terms of what they feel is a moral course of action and what exactly is not moral to them. People's moral identities are socially construed through their affiliation and interaction with specific communities (Bauman, 1993). Moral identity is "self-regulatory mechanism that motivates moral action" (Aquine & Reed, 2002, p. 1423). People who have high levels of moral identity are more likely to engage in ethical and altruistic behaviors (Detert et al., 2008). Research also suggests that contextual cues such as award mechanisms in an organization's culture can influence if people value morality or not (Leavitt et al., 2016). For example, in some subcultures such as within certain organizations or geographic locations, being less moral to achieve desired objectives might be considered as acceptable. However, people have high inherent moral identities and chose to revolt and leave situations when faced with unethical behaviors that do not align with their moral identities (Aquino & Becker, 2005). Thus, it is essential for negotiators to understand who they are negotiating with and what subculture they come from. Although negotiation partners may be from cultures that are perceived as highly moral such as the Japanese, yet negotiators must not forget about the influence of routinized moral standards within individual organizations or subcultures. In such cases, the concept of trustworthiness is highly relevant. If negotiators personally know the negotiators and are aware of their moral identities, such negotiators can be trusted. Also, it is likely that the trusted negotiators will not engage in immoral behaviors as negotiations unfold.

Communication and Intercultural Negotiation

Negotiations are essential processes, and they involve extensive meetings among parties trying to reach a mutually beneficial solution to a problem or an opportunity. Meetings in negotiations comprise of extensive two-way communications wherein each party expresses their opinion or thoughts to other parties. An essential tool for entrepreneurs in intercultural negotiations is adopting communication strategies that are best suited for the situations. We know that in any social interaction, people are motivated to pursue and shape goals as communication with other people unfold (Dillard, 1989). These goals are "future states of affairs that individuals desire to attain or maintain through communication and coordination with others" (Wilson, 2002). We also know that people selectively pursue specific goals based on messages conveyed to them by other parties in negotiation (Berger, 2007). Thus, it is evident that people's choice of goals is dynamic and the communication they have with other people has an impact on the number and type of goals chosen to be pursued.

While communicating, negotiators can either choose competitive or cooperative goals (Liu & Wilson, 2013). When negotiators choose competitive goals, their sole objective is to maximize personal benefit. On the other hand, when negotiators choose cooperative goals, they desire to build relationships and generate solutions that create value for all parties. In an intercultural negotiation, the negotiators must first do their analysis of the perceived culture of other parties in negotiation. Based on the subjective perception of other parties' culture, it is essential to choose the right combination of cooperative or competitive goals. For cross-cultural negotiations, it is essential to have a balance of both cooperative and competitive goals. This way entrepreneurs can make sure that there will be no roadblocks to negotiation progress right at the initiation. As the negotiations unfold, it is a good practice to selectively pursue goals that are either cooperative or competitive. Under situations of resistance from cross-cultural negotiators, it is best to briefly not pursue competitive goals and focus on goals that are welcomed by other negotiators. Willingness to be flexible during the initial stages can help negotiators build rapport among other negotiators even though they are from different cultures or speak different languages and are relatively unknown to each other.

To be able to shape goals based on cultural differences in cross-cultural negotiations, the negotiator must engage in cultural perspective-taking. Cultural perspective-taking is the process of "active consideration of the other party's culturally-normative negotiation behaviors prior to negotiation" (Lee et al., 2013). Culturally normative negotiation behaviors are the ones that are socially appropriate courses of action within particular cultures of consideration. To be able to initially shape interaction goals and modify them in later stages of negotiation process, negotiators must engage in two critical tasks. First, the negotiator must be aware of the norms in the culture of other negotiators. This key information not only shapes their communication but also directs how negotiators must alter their goals later in the process of negotiation. Second, based on the acquisition of cultural norms of other negotiators, it is essential for negotiators to engage in viewing personal interaction goals and the entire process of negotiation wearing the shoes of negotiators from other cultures. Research suggests that when people engage in perspective-taking, it enables them to overcome prejudices and stereotypes (Galinsky et al., 2005). Overcoming prejudices and stereotypes can do wonders in cross-cultural negotiations by facilitating equitable outcomes for all parties in negotiation. Perspective-taking can also act as an icebreaker and facilitate the formation of psychological bonds between people (Galinsky et al., 2005). Becoming comfortable and friendly with negotiators is essential, and perspective-taking can be an excellent tool when there are language barriers that inhibit negotiators to express themselves freely and precisely.

Perspective-taking and shaping interaction goals are precursor to choosing appropriate language for negotiation meetings. Research suggests that when negotiators adopt language style based on perspective-taking, they realize relatively higher levels of mutual benefits (Kern et al., 2014). Language style can be operationalized in many forms and one such form is the type of pronouns used in framing sentences. We know that when people use the pronoun "I," it signals higher levels of social distance from other people (Kuhnen et al., 2001). On the other hand, usage of pronoun such as "You" also reflects social distance but at the same time conveys a signal that the speaker is aware of the distinctiveness of the listener, and the speaker is actively listening (Cheng et al., 2003). Negotiators vary in terms of their experience with different cultures. When negotiators have experience in multiple cultures and use the pronoun "You" more often, social distance between negotiators is lowered thereby leading to elevated mutual gains (Kern et al., 2014). Thus, in cross-cultural negotiation, it is very essential for entrepreneurs to shape their sentences using precise pronouns to facilitate lower social distance from negotiators of other cultures and achieve higher mutual gains.

Role of Emotions in Intercultural Negotiation

As negotiations unfold, negotiators undergo changes in emotional states by numerous factors such as behaviors of other negotiators, communication styles of other negotiators as well as their perceived difficulty to communicate in cross-cultural settings. A key determinant of outcomes of negotiations is the displayed emotions of different people who are actively negotiating with each other (Kopelman & Rosette, 2008). An interesting thing about emotions is that they are contagious, that is, if one person displays the emotion of sadness, people who meet this person are also likely to feel sad (Hatfield et al., 1993). Emotions vary in terms of their valence. They can be broadly classified into positively or negatively valenced emotions. In negotiations, negatively valenced emotions can play a detrimental role. In cross-cultural negotiations it is possible that negotiators vary in terms of importance paid to saving face. Some culture value the importance of saving face, which simply means the importance paid respect, honor, and reputation in public settings (Oetzel et al., 2001). We know that using negative emotions can be useful in some negotiations to extract concessions when the other party has relatively lower bargaining power and fewer alternatives (Sinaceur & Tiedens, 2006). The strategy should generally work except for situations where other party's culture values saving face. Parties who face angry opponents might feel they are being humiliated in public which in turn will most likely lead to conflicts and early termination of negotiations.

It is also essential to note that the type of negative emotions faced by people from individualistic and collectivistic cultures are also different. People from individualistic cultures are more likely to experience emotions such as sadness and despair whereas people from collectivist cultures are more likely to experience emotions such as anxiety and nervousness (Kumar, 2004). The key difference between these emotions is that sadness is a withdrawal emotion whereas anxiety is an approach emotion. When people face withdrawal emotions, they are more likely to escape situations that cause negative emotions. On the other hand, when people experience approach emotions, they are more likely to engage in defensive actions and approach the cause of negative emotions. Thus, in cross-cultural negotiations, the remedy for deleterious outcomes of negative emotions is based on the culture of parties facing such emotions. When negotiators from individualistic cultures face negative emotions, every care must be taken to prevent their withdrawal from negotiations. On the other hand, negotiators must be prepared for backlash from negotiators under influence of negative emotions and hail from collectivist cultures.

Displaying positive emotions in negotiations is also an excellent strategy as they lead to higher levels of cooperation among people (Forgas, 1998). There are instances where negotiating parties are in conflict and are experiencing negative emotions. In such cases, displaying positive emotions can do wonders. Negotiators who display positive emotions after a dispute can achieve future relationships and overcome the negative impact of disputes (Kopelman et al., 2006). Disputes are likely to induce the feeling among negotiators that other parties are indifferent to their needs and are solely interested in maximizing their personal goals. Such instances are very common and a good strategy to overcome such perceptions is through display of compassion. Compassion is an emotion that is focused on other people. People perceive that it is elicited when people are perceptive and attentive to other people's concerns (Markus & Kitayama, 1991). Compassion by itself may not resolve the concerns of other parties, but it can lay foundation for future course of mutual interactions.

Chapter Summary

Culture plays a crucial role in negotiations. With the growing ease of doing business across the world, it is essential for entrepreneurs to understand the role of culture in negotiations. Entrepreneurs can use sound understating of culture to their benefit when shaping cross-cultural negotiation strategies. They must be socially aware of their own culture and understand how their culture differs from culture of business partners they negotiate with. Cultures vary in terms of their relative collectivism/individualism. Entrepreneurs must keep in mind that people negotiate in unique ways such that negotiators from individualistic cultures negotiate in a straightforward manner whereas negotiators from collectivist cultures negotiate indirectly by utilizing contextual cues. It is essential for entrepreneurs from individualistic cultures to not engage in self-serving bias of fairness. When people engage in self-serving bias of fairness, they want to stand out from crowd and blame their failure on others. Such behavior can be perceived as intimidating and condescending by people from collectivist cultures. Before formally entering negotiations, entrepreneurs must make sure to carefully craft their interaction goals. It is also essential for entrepreneurs to engage in evaluating the moral identities of their negotiation counterparts which helps them shape trustworthiness perceptions. Negotiations are social processes, and the role of emotions in negotiations cannot be ignored. Utilization of negative emotions such as anger can lead to varying outcomes based on cultural backgrounds of other parties. Negative emotions can derail negotiations, but they can sometimes generate concessions when other parties do not have many alternatives. Entrepreneurs can use positive emotions to their benefit as they help build social bonds among parties in negotiations.

Key Terms

- Individualistic/collectivist culture
- High-/low-context culture
- Moral identity
- Social awareness
- Self-serving bias
- Interaction goals
- Perspective-taking
- Negative/positive emotions

Case

Lolita is a fashion designer from Los Angeles and has recently started her own clothing brand. Her clothing brand is an instant success in the United States. To expand her business overseas, Lolita decides to enter the markets of Japan. She plans a trip to Tokyo. Her assistant advises her that Japan and Australia have different cultures from the United States and she must prepare in advance for her trips. During her trip, Lolita plans to meet retailers who are willing to carry her products in their stores. Lolita does not know much about the cultures of Japan or Australia but a quick search on the internet revealed that Japanese women's traditional outfit is Kimono and Japan is famous for its sushi. To showcase how seriously she takes the cultural difference, Lolita buys two outfits. One is a Kimono and the other one is a scarf with sushi printed all over. She wears the outfit to her meeting with Japanese retailers. She starts off the meeting by telling everyone in the room how successful she is and how she plans to do great in Japan. About 30 minutes into negotiations, she realizes that the Japanese negotiators are not communicating well and are gazing into their computer screens. She has no clue how to advance negotiations and command the attention of negotiation counterparts. To her surprise, she realizes that some of the negotiators seem upset.

Q. 1 Was Lolita socially aware?
Q. 2 What wrong did Lolita do that led to the awkward situations?
Q. 3 What are possible courses of action available to resolve the tension between Lolita and Japanese retailers?
Q. 4 How would Lolita's action shaped negotiations if she was negotiating with similar retailers within the United States?

References

Adair, W. L. (2003). Integrative sequences and negotiation outcome in same- and mixed-culture negotiations. *International Journal of Conflict Management, 14*(3–4), 273–296.

Aquino, K. F., & Becker, T. E. (2005). Lying in negotiations: How individual and situational factors influence the use of neutralization strategies. *Journal of Organizational Behavior, 26*, 661–679.

Aquino, K., & Reed, A. II. (2002). The self-importance of moral identity. *Journal of Personality and Social Psychology, 83*(6), 1423–1440.

Bauman, Z. (1993). *Postmodern Ethics*. Oxford: Blackwell.

Berger, J. A., & Heath, C. (2007). *Where Consumers Diverge From Others: Identity Signaling and Product Domains*. The Wharton School.

Bilefsky. (2018). Can a Canadian carry off bollywood style? Justin Trudeau finds out. https://www.nytimes.com/2018/02/23/world/canada/trudeaus-bollywood-attire -india.html.

Brett, J. M., & Gelfand, M. J. (2005). *A Cultural Analysis of the Underlying Assumptions of Negotiation Theory*. Palo Alto, CA: Stanford University Press.

Carnevale, P. (1995). Property, culture, and negotiation. In R. Kramer & D. M. Messick (Eds.), *Negotiation as a Social Process*. Newbury Park, CA: Sage.

Chen, J.-H. (2003). A study of the relationship among work values, job stress, and organizational commitment of private senior high school teachers. (Unpublished master's thesis). Changhua, Taiwan: National Changhua University of Education.

Detert, J. R., Treviño, L. K., & Sweitzer, V. L. (2008). Moral disengagement in ethical decision making: A study of antecedents and outcomes. *The Journal of Applied Psychology, 93*(2), 374–391.

Dillard, J. P. (1989). Types of influence goals in personal relationships. *Journal of Social and Personal Relationships, 6*, 293–308.

Forgas, J. P. (1998). On feeling good and getting your way: Mood effects on negotiator cognition and bargaining strategies. *Journal of Personality and Social Psychology, 74*(3), 565–577.

Galinsky, A. D., Ku, G., & Wang, C. (2005). Perspective-taking and self-other overlap: Fostering social bonds and facilitating social coordination. *Group Processes & Intergroup Relations, 8*, 109–124.

Gaspar, J. P., Levine, E. E., & Schweitzer, M. E. (2015). Why we should lie. *Organizational Dynamics, 44*, 306–309.

Ghemawat, P. (2001). Distance still matters: The hard reality of global expansion. *Harvard Business Review, 79*, 137–147.

Hall, E. (1971). 'The paradox of culture'. In B. Landis and E. S. Tauber (Eds.), *In the Name of Life. Essays in Honor of Erich Fromm, New York, 1970*, pp. 218–235. Holt: Rinehart and Winston.

Hatfield, E., Cacioppo, J. T., & Rapson, R. L. (1993). Emotional contagion. *Current Directions in Psychological Science, 2*(3), 96–100.

Heine, S. J., and Lehman, D. R. (1999). 'Culture, self-discrepancies, and self-satisfaction'. *Personality and Social Psychology Bulletin*, Vol. 25, pp. 915–925.

Hofstede, G. (2001). *Culture's consequences: Comparing values, behaviors, institutions, and organizations across nations*, 2nd ed. Thousand Oaks, CA: Sage.

Inman, A. G., & Ladany, N. (2014). Multicultural competencies in psychotherapy supervision.

Kern, M. L., Eichstaedt, J. C., Schwartz, H. A., Park, G., Ungar, L. H., Stillwell, D. J., Kosinski, M., Dziurzynski, L., and Seligman, M. E. (2014). 'From "Sooo excited!!!" to "So proud": Using language to study development'. *Developmental Psychology*, Vol. 50, No. 1, pp. 178–188.

Kopelman, S., & Rosette, A. S. (2008). Cultural variation in response to strategic emotions in negotiations. *Group Decision and Negotiation, 17*(1), 65–77.

Kopelman, S., Rosette, A. S., & Thompson, L. (2006). The three faces of eve: Strategic displays of positive, negative, and neutral emotions in negotiations. *Organizational Behavior and Human Decision Processes, 99*, 81–101.

Kühnen, U., Hannover, B., Roeder, U., Shah, A. A., Schubert, B., Upmeyer, A., & Zakaria, S. (2001). Cross-cultural variations in identifying embedded figures. *Journal of Cross-Cultural Psychology, 32*, 366–372.

Kumar, R. (2004). 'Culture and emotions in intercultural negotiations: An overview'. In M. J. Gelfand and J. M. Brett (Eds.), *The handbook of negotiation and culture*, pp. 95–113. Stanford: Stanford University Press.

Leavitt, K., Zhu, L., & Aquino, K. F. (2016). Good without knowing it: Subtle contextual cues can activate moral identity and reshape moral intuition. *Journal of Business Ethics, 137*, 785–800.

Lee, S., Trimi, S., & Kim, C. (2013). The impact of cultural differences on technology adoption. *Journal of World Business, 48*, 20–29.

Liu, H., Molyneux, P. and Wilson, J. O. (2013). Competition and stability in European banking: A regional analysis. *The Manchester School, 81*, 176–201.

Markus, H. R., & Kitayama, S. (1991). Culture and the self: Implications for cognition, emotion, and motivation. *Psychological Review, 98*, 224–253.

McGinn, K. L. & Croson, R. (2004). What do communication media mean for negotiations: A question of social awareness? In *Handbook of Negotiation and Culture*. Palo Alto, CA: Stanford University Press, pp. 334–349.

Messick, D. M., Bloom, S., Boldizar, J. P., & Samuelson, C. D. (1985). Why we are fairer than others. *Journal of Experimental Social Psychology, 21*(5), 480–500.

Oetzel, J. G., Ting-Toomey, S., Masumoto, T., Yokochi, Y., Pan, X., Takai, J., & Wilcox, R. G. (2001). Face and facework in conflict: A cross-cultural comparison of China, Germany, Japan, and the United States. *Communication Monographs, 68*, 235–258.

Schweitzer, M. E., & Hsee, C. K. (2002). Stretching the truth: Elastic justification and motivated communication of uncertain information. *Journal of Risk and Uncertainty, 25*, 185–201.

Sedikides, C., Campbell, W. K., Reeder, G. D., and Elliot, A. J. (1998). 'The self-serving bias in relational context'. *Journal of Personality and Social Psychology*, Vol. 74, No. 2, pp. 378–386.

Sinaceur, M., & Tiedens, L. Z. (2006). Get mad and get more than even: When and why anger expression is effective in negotiations. *Journal of Experimental Social Psychology, 42*(3), 314–322.

Steinel, W. (2015). Social value orientation and deception: Are proselfs liars? *Current Opinion in Psychology, 6*, 211–215.

Triandis, H. C., & Vassiliou, V. (1972). Interpersonal influence and employee selection in two cultures. *Journal of Applied Psychology, 56*(2), 140–145.

Urban, M. S., & Witt, L. A. (1990). Self-serving bias in group member attributions of success and failure. *Journal of Social Psychology, 130*, 417–418.

Wilson, M. (2002). Six views of embodied cognition. *Psychonomic Bulletin & Review, 9*, 625–636.

INDEX